# THE PROBLEM

# OF RACE

# IN THE

# TWENTY-FIRST

# CENTURY

THE NATHAN I. HUGGINS LECTURES

# THE PROBLEM
# OF RACE
# IN THE
# TWENTY-FIRST
# CENTURY

## THOMAS C. HOLT

HARVARD UNIVERSITY PRESS

CAMBRIDGE, MASSACHUSETTS

LONDON, ENGLAND

2000

Library of Congress Cataloging-in-Publication Data

Holt, Thomas C. (Thomas Cleveland), 1942–
The problem of race in the twenty-first century / Thomas C. Holt.
    p.    cm. — (The Nathan I. Huggins lectures)
Includes bibliographical references.
ISBN 0-674-00443-4
1. Race.   2. Racism.   I. Title.   II. Series.
HT1521.H585 2000
305.8—dc21
00-057238

FOR

SHOSHANA MICHAELA (B. 1999)

AND IN MEMORY OF

GROVER CLEVELAND HOLT (1917–2000)

# Contents

# Preface

This book began with a paper I prepared some years ago that bore the rather formidable title "How will we explain race in the twenty-first century?" and that I presented in lecture form to graciously responsive audiences at Memphis State University and as the Herbert G. Gutman Memorial lecturer at the City University of New York. I am grateful to Kenneth Goings at Memphis State and Judith Mara Gutman at CUNY for providing those opportunities to try out and develop my ideas. In time I thought better of the title, fearing that audiences might expect me to deliver a definitive answer rather than just another set of hard questions. My question about the future was in fact a heuristic device reflecting the historian's faith that understanding the past is essential in preparing for the future. Thus when I had an opportunity to deliver a revised version of the paper in 1997, first to the Race and the Reproduction of Racial Ideologies Workshop at the University of Chicago and then to a conference, Racializing Class and Classifying Race, hosted by Oxford University, I changed the title to its present noninterrogative form. I am grateful to the auditors and readers in both venues for their sharp and probing questions.

These experiences made it clear that the many themes and problems raised in my talk and in followup questions could not be adequately covered in a single lecture. An invitation from Henry Louis Gates Jr. and his colleagues at the W. E. B. Du Bois Institute at Harvard University to deliver a series of three lectures presented a welcome opportunity to expand upon those themes and questions. Even so, the material constantly threatened to burst the acceptable time limits for a reasonable-length talk. Consequently, although the themes are the same, this book differs in many respects from the lectures: it not only includes more material but also responds to challenging questions from the audience.

This work has benefited immensely from questions and commentary from various readers. My wife Leora Auslander has given me innumerable helpful suggestions, a few of which are acknowledged in the notes, and generally encouraged me to think that this was not a fool's errand. My sincere thanks to friends and colleagues, Julie Saville, Rebecca J. Scott, and Jean-Claude Zancarini, who took time from their own work to help me with mine. Equally crucial to the development of this book have been the many students in my undergraduate and graduate classes on race and racism, first at the University of Michigan and lately at the University of Chicago. The skepticism of the undergraduates toward professorial pronouncements has been salutary, while the impact of the work of the graduates is indicated by my numerous citations of their dissertations and forthcoming books. Aida Donald, my editor at Harvard University Press, facilitated the rapid transition from lectures to a book. Ann Hawthorne, my manuscript editor, gently and firmly helped me turn "lecture-speak" into readable prose.

I have received time and space to work on this project through generous support from the Center for Advanced Study in the Behavioral Sciences in Stanford, California, where I began this project, and the John F. Kennedy-Institut für Nordamerikastudien at the Freie Universität in Berlin, where I completed it. I am especially grateful to the latter institution's director, Knud Krakau, and to Professor Willi Paul Adams for their gracious hospitality and assistance at a critical juncture. My academic leaves have been supported financially by the University of Chicago's Social Science Division and History Department. Finally, over the years I have received important research assistance from current and former students, Steve Essig, Laurie Green, and Hannah Rosen.

The year that bracketed the culmination of this project also marked the birth of my third daughter and the death of my father. Much of this book is about the crucial transformation occurring during my father's life and times; undoubtedly much of what I know and say has been shaped by his reflections on those times. My daughter's birth, practically on the eve of this new century, deepened and intensified the concerns that underlay those reflections, given my growing awareness that the future I write about will be hers.

*Berlin*
*May 2000*

# THE PROBLEM

# OF RACE

# IN THE

# TWENTY-FIRST

# CENTURY

# Introduction:
# Race, Culture,
# and History

At the dawn of the twentieth century, W. E. B. Du Bois made a prediction that remains astonishing in its perceptiveness and relevance: "The problem of the twentieth century," he wrote, "is the problem of the color-line,—the relations of the darker to the lighter races of men in Asia and Africa, in America and the islands of the sea."[1] And indeed issues of group difference—and especially *racialized* differences—have informed most of the major conflicts of the century.

Du Bois's prophecy was necessarily based largely on the nineteenth-century world in which he was born and came of age—a world of colonialism and imperialism, crude labor exploitation, the rise of virulent racist ideologies, and lynching. But within that scenario Du Bois also discerned newer forces, in particular a virtually unchallenged materialism and its desiccation of the human spirit. One of the main themes of his 1903 book, *Souls of Black Folk,* was a challenge to the emerging monopoly-capitalist world order that sought to make material self-interest the primary value of human existence. His prophecy, then, was grounded in his analysis of his past and keen observation of his present.

One might well ask, at the beginning of the twenty-first century, whether we could do as well. Given our understanding of the world in which we have come of age and our reading of our future on the basis of our present existence, what kind of role can we predict that race will play in that future? And if we are unable to offer such an analysis, what does that very inability suggest about our confidence in that future? What does it suggest about our ability to plot a course of resistance and reformation? What is our ability to imagine solutions?

Will the concepts and tools we have developed for understanding the racism of the nineteenth and twentieth centuries be adequate for the twenty-first? Should we even expect them to be? I think not; and here I will attempt to offer both reasons why not and some suggestions about the issues and factors we must consider if we are to reframe our analyses of racial phenomena in such a way as to make them more adequately reflect the future world(s) we are in the process of making.

Why is the way we are accustomed to thinking about race and racism inadequate to the evolving world? In popular and academic discourse, racism is conventionally understood to refer to the hostility one group feels toward another on the basis of the alleged biological and/or cultural inferiority of that other. Among its manifestations are exploitation of the labor and/or property of that other (as in slavery and colonialism), exclusion of that other from participation in public life and institutions (as in segregation and disfranchisement), and massive physical violence against that other (as in lynching). There is no doubt that all these phenomena continue to characterize relations among racialized groups in America and elsewhere. I would argue, however, that such phenomena do not capture all aspects of the contemporary situation and, more importantly, may miss significant changes under way. There are *new* anomalies, *new* ambiguities, and a *new* ambivalence in contemporary life that our standard definitions of race and racism simply cannot account for, and which even render them somewhat anachronistic.[2]

To begin with one of the more familiar and recent of these anomalies, we had in America just recently a situation wherein a black man, Colin Powell, could be seriously and credibly considered as a viable Republican challenger for the presidency. The point here is not whether he might have won or not—there is plenty of room for skepticism about that[3]—but rather that the very idea of his successfully contesting the presidential election was not received with overwhelming scorn or patronizing sounds as had been the case just a decade before, when Jesse Jackson first ran for the Democratic nomination. Instead, mere speculation about a Powell candidacy was met with plans by monied men to raise the considerable funds needed to wage a successful presidential campaign.[4]

On one level, this development could—perhaps even does—represent real change in both white attitudes and the racial climate of this country. But what is most interesting about the Powell phenomenon is its anomalous relationship to the conditions of life and the life chances of most black people. Indeed, even while speculation about whether a black former military officer of the highest rank would run for president was most intense, other members of that same military brutally murdered a black couple in

North Carolina. We learned later that these murders were part of a ritual initiation into one of the neo-Nazi cells organized on many military bases.[5] The arbitrariness, the randomness, the casualness of this snuffing out of black life evokes memories of the high tide of lynching in the 1890s; it suggests racial regression, not progress.

One response to this anomaly might be simply to dismiss the phenomenon of Powell's potential electability as president as chimerical, to say—as many blacks indeed do—that *nothing* has changed. I believe that view is as wrong and shortsighted as thinking that the millennium of racial peace is just around the corner. What are not to be missed in this scenario are its contradictions and incoherence; like a cracked mirror portraying a fragmented image, "all odds and evens." What we need to explain are why and how Powell's credibility as a presidential candidate and the North Carolina murders can coexist. The simultaneous idealization of Colin Powell and demonization of blacks as a whole (especially the politically motivated demonization of large numbers of black women as "welfare queens" by members of Powell's own party) is replicated in much of our everyday world.

Reflect for a moment on an admittedly fictional—though fact-based—scenario. What if the rock music star Michael Jackson, at the height of his popularity a few years ago, had visited one of the all-white neighborhoods of New York City or Chicago? He almost certainly would have been met by screaming, wild mobs of white youths.

They would have been screaming their adoration of him and his music. If they had torn his clothing, the objective would have been to get a valuable trophy from a living icon of American popular culture. Fast-forward to a few weeks later. A black man answering an ad offering a car for sale or a young black male on his bicycle ventures into that same neighborhood. The crowd that welcomed Michael Jackson gathers again. It is screaming. But this time, it screams for blood.[6]

We don't have to look far for more such narratives of contradiction and incoherence in contemporary racial phenomena. I cite these two—one from the world of high politics and one from the everyday world of popular culture—merely to suggest the broad terrain of the problematic I wish to address. We need to begin rethinking our explanations of race, because such phenomena raise profound questions about how we are to recognize racism and the racial, about what kinds of transformations are currently under way in the racial regime we inhabit, and thus about how we are to fashion a response.

## Recognizing Race and Racism

Much contemporary commentary on race and racism seems directed at containing these concepts within fairly narrow and clearly recognizable frames. Indeed, some of these analyses appear more concerned to limit the scope of available legal remedies by narrowly (and anachronistically) defining what can legitimately be called "racially motivated." Others are well-intentioned efforts by careful scholars trying to get a clear "fix" on the object of study; for them, admitting all manner of invidious acts of distinction under a racial designation risks losing focus and analytic efficacy.[7] However, it is clear that a great number of palpably race-related phenomena in contemporary life cannot be comprehended within definitions that seek to sustain such sharp distinctions.

Perhaps part of the problem in contemporary analyses of race is that they address their subject head-on: that is, they begin by attempting to define the concept and to catalogue its substantive content. This approach encounters problems at both ends of the analytic spectrum. Defining racism in terms of the old idea of biological inferiority, for example, leaves unaddressed a lot of patently racist practices in contemporary life. Moreover, we quickly discover in such a catalogue that some of the same ideas and tropes have circulated through racist discourse from time immemorial, a fact that leaves us just a short step away from conceiving racism as a timeless or innate human quality. On the other hand, such a catalogue necessarily entails trying to corral or contain a concept that by its very nature is parasitic and chameleonlike.

In the following pages I hope to show not only that such ambiguous boundaries and seeming atemporality have characterized race and the racial for a very long time—perhaps even since its inception—but also that these very features explain much of its staying power. This undertaking requires that we first reexamine a few of the key concepts or terms—race and racism, culture and ethnicity—used in most discussions of race and on which many such discussions inevitably founder. Though much used, these terms are not always deployed in quite the same way. In each case we tend to assume that we know "it" when we see it. But often the boundaries between the concepts get fuzzier the closer we approach them. Part of the ambiguity of the conception of racism is traceable, certainly, to the ambiguities in the basic language we deploy.

The firing line of this discursive struggle for many of us who teach courses on race is our first class meeting every year. And there the stakes are enormous, because I find each generation of students increasingly pessimistic about the prospects for progress on the question of race. It is pessimism, I am convinced, that arises not from some growing conservatism but from how they conceptualize the racial problematic itself.

Typically I begin that first class by asking for definitions of some of the basic concepts we will engage throughout the course, the most obvious and primary being that of race itself. Much contemporary scholarship begins with the premise that race is a socially constructed entity.[8] Although in many ways that characterization is correct, perhaps the most striking features of contemporary discourse on race—whether in popular or academic circles—are how little of that "academic wisdom" has penetrated discussions outside the university and how quickly academics themselves fall back into the older habits of thought. Part of the reason for this may well be that the discourse of "social constructedness" has an air of unreality about it that may limit its influence. It may be that our own general failure to probe beyond the mantra of social constructedness, to ask what that really might mean in shaping lived experience, bears some responsibility for the shallowness both of the conception itself and of its repudiation in ordinary discourse.

Certainly this state of affairs was reflected in my classes when I first started teaching courses on the subject more than a decade ago. The typical answers I received to the basic question—what is race?—entailed to some extent or other the notion of biology, of physical difference. The task of the discussion thus became one of deconstructing that idea, of showing that it doesn't really work. I would patiently point out that although biological features— whether defined in phenotypic or genetic terms—may be the markers of race, they cannot and do not do the actual work of racial differentiation and distinction. I am classified as black because my skin is dark; in fact my skin is sometimes (especially after a brief stint in sunny regions) almost dark brown, but for most of the year—especially since I have lived and worked in Chicago—it is a rather ashy brown. But there is within my extended family—on my paternal grandmother's side—a branch of the family many of whose members are indistinguishable from what is usually defined as a "white" phenotype, thanks to the lusts of a Virginia slavemaster. How came *they* to be classified as black? A classification based on color alone does not account for one part of my family, then, even if I concede that it roughly fixes me in the phenotypic order of things.

It is here that the other prong of the biological definition of race is invoked: genetics. Races are defined as sharing a common gene pool, one that predisposes them to certain physical tendencies like hair and eye color and body type. Such a definition has the aura of scientific objectivity and solidity; it comports with much of our common knowledge about our bodies. After all, we know that even the predisposition to certain diseases and medical conditions, like sickle cell, Tay-Sachs, or lactose intolerance, can be traced racially. But even here biology has difficulty doing the work generally required of it in racial discourse. It needs help. "Race" spills over its boundaries. Common gene pools arise and are sustained in the first place because of the endogamous mating practices of a given population, which are in turn the consequence of geographic isolation, social or political restrictions on mating outside the group, and so forth. In short, gene pools don't decide by themselves that they "share" something.

Thus a racial category—often presented as given and constitutive—is instead itself dependent on myriad other variables. Moreover, those variables, the forces that sustain it, are social, not biological; and when those forces weaken or break down—as in population migrations, interracial social contacts, or changes in laws and social practices—the biological basis for race is also weakened or breaks down. One episode of interracial mating puts in doubt the whole edifice of racial differentiation—as happened to the family of my paternal grandmother, the Waltons. After that slavemaster's one night of pleasure, it took all the king's horses and all the king's men to make the Waltons black. Biology could not be relied upon to do the job anymore. It took antimiscegenation laws, census takers, a vigilant state Bureau of Vital Statistics that aggressively enforced racial boundaries in issuing birth certificates and marriage licenses,[9] job discrimination, separate school systems, and . . . if all else failed, bloodhounds and lynch mobs. All that to keep the white-skinned Waltons . . . black.

With that personal anecdote I was able to convey with concreteness and immediacy the principal arguments made in an impressive and growing academic literature on this subject. And if I was lucky I could convince my students to look more skeptically on the arguments not only of the less enlightened but also of a lot of smart historians and social scientists who inadvertently slip into arguing that there is a biological basis for racism, even as they generally accept the idea of the social construction of race.[10]

In recent years I've had fewer opportunities to tell that little family story, because my students are much less likely to say that race is biologically determined, or at least to say so out loud. Even if they don't know the academic lingo, they know that "race" is "socially constructed." They know that it arises from social conventions, from agreed-upon fictions that paper over complexities like those I have just described. These are fictions not in the sense of being unreal or untrue, but in the sense of being an agreed-upon set of understandings that may be deployed both by those within the designated group as well as by those outside it. After all, it also suited the Waltons' purposes to embrace their racial designation as black. Blackness was in many ways "home"—it connected them to a particular community, to institutions, to a culture and an identity. For different reasons and motives, then, "the fiction" to this day is sustained on both sides of the racial divide. On which side of that racial divide one fell was biologically arbitrary, but no less real. Of course, we understand all this without really or fully internalizing it. I am black because I am descended from black people— notwithstanding the fact that some of them were actually white. However much we acknowledge the fiction, traces of the old biological idea linger.[11]

But even as we speak the new language of social construction and displace biology from its historically privileged place in definitions of race, we tend to substitute another ambiguous and fraught concept—culture. This substitution—which has characterized much racial thinking in the past half-century—is related to another that

Etienne Balibar remarked on some years ago; there is, he observed, a "new racism" abroad, "a racism without races," in which culture takes on the function previously fulfilled by biology. "It is a racism whose dominant theme is not biological heredity but the insurmountability of cultural differences, a racism which, at first sight, does not postulate the superiority of certain groups or peoples in relation to others but 'only' the harmfulness of abolishing frontiers, the incompatibility of life-styles and traditions."[12]

Though generally persuasive, Balibar may have overstated the case, misreading to some extent a kind of discursive sleight of hand. It is clear that through the "culture" concept biology in fact often reasserts itself. Conceptually culture sustains an aura of voluntarism and mutability that biology forecloses, but in the practical discourse of ordinary folk it carries much the same signification. Indeed, today, more often than not, we use "race" and "culture" as synonyms. We say "black culture," for example, when we really mean to designate African Americans as a group subject to racialized definitions and discipline. We speak of fostering multicultural curriculums and institutions, when we really mean achieving more representation of people of African-American, Latino, or Asian descent and experiences.

But like race, culture carries a conceptual weight it can't quite sustain. For while it is true that each of these groups has one or more cultures that differ from the

mainstream in some respect, most also share and partici-
pate quite extensively in the larger culture. All we need to
do is to go to another country, or even to the country of
our putative cultural origins, to realize this in an instant.
African Americans in Ghana or Nigeria or Korean Americans in South Korea will quickly discover—and be told
quite forcefully, perhaps even during the cab ride from
the airport—that they are *very* American.

Part of the problem here lies in an imprecision of our
concepts of culture that is quite similar to the fuzziness of
our conceptions of race. In our everyday practice—as distinct from academic discourse—we *recognize* culture in
different cuisines, styles of dress, language styles, music,
and even values, but *defining* culture is much more complicated—even for those who earn their living doing just that.
Anthropology fell on hard times as a coherent discipline in
large part because its practitioners became increasingly
uncertain as to just what culture is.[13] Is it institutions, behaviors, or ideas that constitute a culture? Perhaps it is all
of these, articulated in some complex pattern.

Even without waiting for the anthropologists to sort
that all out, it is clear that we cannot think of culture as
simply a set of voluntaristic social practices that we easily
opt into or out of. Indeed, some of the most useful work
on culture for our purposes has been done by those who
keep in view its material base while emphasizing its fundamentally contingent nature.[14] Culture is symbols and
meanings, but there are also powerful institutional ar-

rangements and structures that shape the ways we negotiate our daily routines. Today we live in an advanced capitalist, market economy that dictates a particular array of
behaviors and attitudes and worldview. We drive cars,
watch TV, and are bombarded with similar advertise-
ments and music. Our physical and iconographic environments frame a common psychic template on which we
develop our understandings of ourselves, of the world,
and of how the world works. Whatever their putative racial or ethnic identity, the inhabitants of Western late-
capitalist societies confront powerful forces that dictate
allegiance to the same fundamental culture, notwithstanding variations on or even occasional opposition to
its main themes. Thus the culture concept abuts "the social" and "the ideological," which produces its own ambiguities, leaving it no more capable of doing the work race
requires than biology.

And, of course, the shift from biology to culture has
opened another can of worms for defining the concept of
race. Many analysts attempt to draw a distinction between
an "ethnic" and a "racial" identity and in the process
imply (or assert) that there is a kind of "naturalness," a socially and culturally grounded quality to ethnicity that is
somehow missing from race. Implicitly, and sometimes
explicitly, this distinction appears to arise from the as-
sumption that race is biological and thus suspect, while
ethnicity is cultural and thus valid. Otherwise careful
scholars seem to place implicit quotation marks around

race but not around ethnicity. All this not only tends to confine racial phenomena to a narrower terrain but may also seem to lend greater legitimacy and rationality to ethnically motivated conflicts.[15]

This distinction between ethnicity and race is curious, given the similar etymologies and histories of the terms. Although "race" is an older term than "ethnicity," both have had tortuous, mutable, sometimes overlapping histories. "Ethnicity" is in fact a term coined within my lifetime, if not yours.[16] "Ethnic" is much older, but it also carried a different meaning from the one it usually takes on in contemporary discourse. In fact its etymology drips with irony: a Greek translation of a Hebrew word—*goyim*, the plural for foreign nations or peoples. For Jews it referred to Gentiles, non-Jews, the Other. Later it sustained this connotation even in the mouths of Christians, as it came to designate the non-Christian, the heathen, the pagan, the primitive.[17] By this route "ethnology" and "ethnography" came in the mid-nineteenth century to designate the study of primitive peoples. In fact, by the nineteenth century the term "ethnic" is found in both English and French dictionaries coupled with "race" as one of its synonyms. And of course to this day it remains coupled with race as if an interchangeable part of a single unit—as in "race and ethnicity." But ethnological history and discursive practice aside, ethnic is also used as something different from race. Race is something blacks have; ethnicity belongs to whites.

A number of scholars have exposed the mistaken notion that ethnicity is a social given rather than a social construction, rendering the putative distinctions between ethnicity and race fuzzier still.[18] Some are now busily documenting James Baldwin's prescient if acidic observation in an article in *Essence* a number of years ago: ethnicities, including whiteness itself, had to be created, had literally to be *made up* in the new social environment of America.[19]

### Historicizing Race and Racism

Both race and culture, then, share ambiguous boundaries, and both race and ethnicity are socially constructed identities. Once we have recognized this we immediately confront the fact that both must also be historically contingent. And if they are historical, then their further analysis requires mapping the relations of power, the patterns of contestation and struggle out of which such social constructions emerged.[20] There is no question, then, of defining race and racism (or, for that matter, ethnicity) and following them as unchanging entities through time. It is rather a question of seeing how historical forces shape and change the meanings of these terms over time and space.

Of course, such an approach runs against the persistent image of racism as autonomous from time and place, an idea that is an even more tenacious trope in racial discourse than the stubborn biological idea. There are two seemingly contradictory but interrelated pieces to this: that racism is an anachronistic hangover from some primitive past, and that racism is indeed *timeless*. To pose the question of the origins of racism, therefore, is to invite utterly *a*historical responses. I was told recently at an international historical conference—and by a well-respected, rather famous historian—that racism essentially had no history. Human beings have always drawn invidious distinctions among themselves, he said, and always would. End of story.[21]

If we take that perspective on the subject, we not only cannot locate a temporal beginning point for racism, but its origins in a causal sense are also rendered ahistorical. The causes of racism come to be located in the seemingly natural, universal tendencies of the human species to draw group boundaries, to define who's inside and who's outside those boundaries, to treat the outsider, the stranger differently from those who are somehow "kin." So, racism, like sin and the poor, has always been and always will be.

But even as we move beyond notions of primordiality and innateness (what we might consider relatively uninformed, unreflective views of the matter), the failure to historicize the problem of race lingers on, even in some of the best work on the subject. But if race is socially and historically constructed, then racism must be *re*constructed as social regimes change and histories unfold. Much less attention has been devoted to this problem in racial studies.[22] It is a problem linked to the difficulty we have explaining racism's seeming intractability—or, perhaps to put the matter more accurately, its reproduction. The question, then, is what enables racism to reproduce itself even after the historical conditions that initially gave it life have disappeared? And if we are to sustain an argument about its essential mutability, its historically contingent nature, how do we explain the seemingly endless repetitions of certain stereotypes (they are oversexed), dogmas (they won't work), and images (the lazy, chicken-stealing Sambos).

Part of the solution is to adopt a conception of historical transformation, in which we recognize that a new historical construct is never entirely new and the old is never entirely supplanted by the new. Rather the new is grafted onto the old. Thus racism, too, is never entirely new. Shards and fragments of its past incarnations are embedded in the new. Or, if we switch metaphors to an archaeological image, the new is sedimented onto the old, which occasionally seeps or bursts through. Our problem then, is to figure out how this happens and to take its measure.[23]

The relevant measures reflect neither a temporal antiquity nor a causal innateness. If we are to make sense of racial phenomena in our own era, we must recognize its temporal modernity and its links with essentially modern phenomena, processes, and institutions.

## SOCIAL FORMATIONS AND RACIAL REGIMES

Two decades have passed since Stuart Hall urged that in our attempts to make sense of racial phenomena we "must deal with the historical specificity of race in the modern world."[24] That injunction encourages us to follow through on the implications of the current academic consensus that race and racism are socially constructed. The idea that race is socially constructed implies also that it can and must be constructed differently at different historical moments and in different social contexts. And one of the implications of taking seriously this historicity of race—that there are historically specific "racisms" and not a singular ahistorical racism—is the analytic necessity of exploring how racial phenomena articulate with other social phenomena.[25] As Hall put it: "one cannot explain racism in abstraction from other social relations."[26]

Implicit in this approach is the conviction that neither race nor racism can live independently of its social environments, the times and spaces it inhabits. By nature a changeling, it attaches itself to and draws sustenance from other social phenomena and from racist discourse itself, like one of those insidious monsters in late-night science-fiction movies. The historian is left to examine the carcass it once inhabited before moving on to another social body, while the sociologist busily constructs diagnostic questionnaires after the disease has already mutated.

In invoking these images I confess to being wholly mischievous but only half in jest. Racial phenomena and their meaning do change with time, with history, and with the conceptual and institutional spaces that history unfolds. More specifically they are responsive to major shifts in a political economy and to the cultural systems allied with that political economy. Thus Du Bois could readily see in the 1930s that the fight against racism must deploy differently in the era of monopoly capital and the consumer revolution of the early twentieth century than it had in the world of his youth and coming of age.[27] We must likewise recognize a similar mutation in the globalized economy and even more complex consumption regime at the beginning of the twenty-first century.

Starting from these premises, I will argue that the meaning of race and the nature of racism articulate with (perhaps even are defined by) the given social formation of a particular historical moment. By "social formation" I mean all the interrelated structures of economic, political, and social power, as well as the systems of signification (that is, cultural systems) that give rise to and/or reflect those structures. Thus in my use of the term I am borrowing some aspects of what Pierre Bourdieu has called a *habitus*.[28] For ultimately I wish to focus on a set of linked social relations that are neither wholly determined nor wholly voluntarist. For example, the democratic revolutions of the late eighteenth and early nineteenth centuries gave rise not simply to new political structures and relations, but to economic, social, and cultural relations and phenomena that in turn made possible and necessary new social relations between men and other men, between men and women, between parents and children. It is not necessary to think of such systems as total, closed, complete, or uncontested to understand their pervasive power. It follows, I will argue, that race relations, to the extent that they figure in the political economy of a given social formation, tend to follow the logic of that formation.

In order to provide a basis for exploring what is different about the racial regime of our own day, and possibly of our immediate future, in the following pages I will elaborate three such systems or social formations, their *habitus,* and the racial regimes associated with them. For lack of better nomenclature, I call these the pre-Fordist regime, the Fordist regime, and the post-Fordist regime.[29] The Fordist regime takes its name from Henry Ford's Detroit assembly line and spans the period from the early twentieth century to the recession and debt crisis of the early 1970s (sometimes dated even more specifically to the oil shock of 1973 or to the abandonment of the Bretton Woods global financial system in 1972).[30] This is, of course, our recent history, the era that most directly shaped our present world. The post-Fordist era is the one that we now inhabit and wish to explain; it began in the 1970s and stretches into an indeterminate future. The word "post" signals its ambiguity: different from what preceded it, but not yet fully formed or knowable.

The period preceding the Fordist regime is not at all ambiguous but simply sprawling and unwieldy. Beginning in the sixteenth century and ending sometime between the 1890s and the First World War, it is the period in which much of our current understanding of race and racism is grounded. But drawing our conceptions of race and racism from this very different historical era in our efforts to explain the racial phenomena of our own time can mislead us about how racism works and the sources of resistance to it.

Of course, many scholars have given voice to these or similar concepts and worked them through in various ways. What is often missing in these analyses, however (and I include my own previous work in this criticism), is a historical perspective of sufficient breadth to contextualize adequately the many protean insights developed. Our one consolation about this failing is that we are in good company. Even Du Bois, whom we might well call the dean of modern race studies, fell prey to this limitation. His famous prophecy—"the problem of the twentieth century is the problem of the color-line"—which began an essay on the Freedmen's Bureau and its role in mediating the transition from slavery to freedom after the Civil War, grew out of reflections on his past and present, but at the time Du Bois did not follow up his prophetic insight with a systematic analysis of its import. On the other hand, by framing his prophecy with a close study of the past, Du Bois pioneered an approach that we might do well to emulate. The question about how racial phenomena will be configured in the future is also a question about where we have been and where we are.

# 1

# Racial Identity and the Project of Modernity

I have suggested that the tropes of racism are fairly constant whereas the repertoire of racist practices is all too mutable. Recognizing the relative plasticity of race and racism as concepts and their parasitic and chameleonlike qualities as practice, I have also suggested that we might do better *not* to try to define or catalogue their content. Rather, our task might be instead to ask what *work* race does. In this I am consciously following up on Stuart Hall's insight, some two decades old now, that race is "the modality in which class is 'lived,' the medium through which class relations are experienced, the form in which it is appropriated and 'fought through.' "[1] If one pushes that insight beyond the race-class dynamic per se, there is the clear implication that other forms of our social relations also have work for race to do.

Perhaps in the word "work" we can convey the dynamism and contingency of phenomena that other descriptors might render flat and ahistorical. In doing its "work" race articulates with (in the sense of relating to) and sometimes articulates for (in the sense of speaking for) other social phenomena, like class, gender, and nationality. And through that articulation—in all its forms—it often achieves social effects that mask its own presence, or the presence of other forces, like class. Sometimes transforming other social categories, sometimes itself transformed by them, race can seem either to be all or not to be present at all.[2]

Race is ideological, but, being embedded in political economies that are quite historically specific, it cannot long survive changes in the material base from which it draws sustenance. Such changes necessarily portend changes in how, as Hall phrases it, the modality of race is lived, is struggled through. Accordingly, my first main task will be to trace the origins and development of race and racism within one historically specific political-economic regime, and to show how in the course of that development it both shaped and was shaped by another major emergent social phenomenon—the modern nation-state. Race articulates with the terms on both sides of that hyphen. The struggle for state power and the deployment of that power to racial ends is perhaps the most familiar of these connections. The less familiar story, perhaps, is how race articulates with nation, both in drawing the boundaries of national identity and in the closely related but slightly different task of national formation. In each of these domains race has a profound resonance with changes under way in our own era, suggesting that it is neither an irrational anachronism nor near the end of the work it can do.

## The Pre-Fordist Regime

The pre-Fordist regime is the most unwieldy of the eras in this longue-durée history of racial phenomena. Though ungainly it encompasses the beginning and ending of a fundamental social-historical transformation with which race is linked: modern forms of politics, economy, social life, culture, and consciousness unfolded in this era. Race and racism as we know them also took shape in this period, as did critical social forms and identities with which they would be forever linked. In both its timing and its associations, therefore, race is a thoroughly modern phenomenon, indelibly linked to the evolution of modern institutions, modern sensibilities, and a modern consciousness.[3]

Race is linked to modernity first in the fact that racializing institutions—like the slave plantation—are thoroughly modern in form and function; in the fact that racial thought shares with other modern forms of knowledge a "disenchantment" of the world; and finally, in the fact that modernity produces social and psychic conditions for which racial knowledge appears to offer a solution.

Modernity, of course, is another much-debated concept, with disputes as to its content and precise temporal boundaries. But these disputes need not detain us here. It is clear enough that there were transformations in how humans thought, lived, and negotiated their place in the world—the intellectual, the economic, the political—that can be persuasively grouped under the rubric "modernity." No doubt the incongruous timing of these different modalities of modernity gives rise to some of its conceptual ambiguity; arguably the intellectual transformation came earliest, the political latest, and the economic spanned the whole period.[4] Suffice it to say that each of these modalities contributed to fundamental changes in worldview; and I mean quite literally—changes in how the world was viewed.

The modern era, one marked by an intensification of physical and social contacts on a global scale, necessitated a different way of seeing the most mundane aspects of everyday living. In the sixteenth century the world enlarged and grew infinitely more complex. At this long remove we can scarcely begin to imagine what it must have meant for peoples long in relative isolation to have come into sudden, and over time extraordinarily intimate, relations with other worlds.[5]

Economically, the modern world as we know it grew out of European exploration and geographic expansion and was consolidated with the expansion of capitalist social relations in the late eighteenth and early nineteenth centuries. Scholars like W. E. B. Du Bois, C. L. R. James, and Eric Williams have shown from various angles of vision that the histories of European capitalist expansion, which is so crucial to the development of the modern world and modernity, cannot be fully understood without acknowledgment of the central role of Africans, and specifically of Africans in the Americas.[6] Du Bois suggested that the African slave trade established the first truly global markets of exchange. Eric Williams drew our attention to the credit markets and financial infrastructures that developed with that trade. And C. L. R. James was among the first to suggest how intimately European politics, revolutions, and even the idea of freedom itself were bound up with slavery in the Americas and sometimes even—as in the Haitian Revolution in the 1790s—with slaves' revolutionary initiatives.[7]

In recent years others have built on that scholarship to describe a formative era in which political, economic, and cultural linkages were forged principally among Europe, Africa, and the Americas; three regions that formed a space at once physical and conceptual—an Atlantic world. In sum, we now appreciate the degree to which transatlantic slavery and the slave trade marked one of those historic ruptures in human relations that redefined the very conditions of possibility for production and consumption, forms of labor mobilization, the shape of revolution and reaction, as well as fundamental notions of personal and political identity.[8] We have come to see how Europe was remade through these contacts as surely as were the indigenous civilizations it encountered in Africa, America, and Asia. Slave-grown sugar, cotton, and tobacco changed how Europeans fed and clothed themselves, and even how they worked and spent their leisure time.[9]

Finally, the global linkages within that world, first fashioned through slavery and the slave trade, were reconstructed and modified with slave emancipation and the evolution of postemancipation labor regimes, with colonial and anticolonial social developments, and with twentieth-century liberation movements.[10] And, of course, race and racism were thus remade with each of these moments of transformation.

My point here is not that people did not harbor prejudices against each other before the sixteenth century, hate each other before, even kill each other for reasons of group differences that often took on a racial character.[11] What was new was that racialized labor forces became crucial to the mobilization of productive forces on a world scale. Even in the late nineteenth and early twentieth centuries, as slave regimes were destroyed or receded, the global configurations they had wrought continued to frame ideologies of work and citizenship, systems of labor mobilization and exploitation, and diverse claims for participation in the modern world.[12] Moreover, other regions were brought within this system through the recruitment of contract laborers from India and China, which completed the systems' global reach.

In many ways, then, this pre-Fordist era prefigured many aspects of the post-Fordist era, discussed later, in that these global systems promoted broad similarities in the ways in which people chose or were forced to live their lives. One cannot understand issues of identity and difference, therefore, absent that political-economic context.

But the modernity of race was not defined only by the critically important role that racialized labor regimes played in the emergent political economies of the Atlantic world. In brief, the "work" race did should not be conflated with the work blacks did. Race articulated with the very project of modernity, a project whose essence was to make sense of a world in which humankind was both the object of knowledge and the ultimate author of knowledge.[13] And, by all accounts, these twin moves toward secular authority and the secularization of knowledge were enabling for racist ideologies.[14] It is no accident that the image of the grand classifiers, like Linnaeus, is stamped on the birth of the modern temperament. Indeed, classification and inductive reasoning are among the dominant themes of modernity. Perhaps it is no accident either that this occurred as Europeans came into more intimate contact with the peoples of Africa and the Americas.[15] And it is certainly no accident that this age of discovery was characterized by the construction of elaborate hierarchical systems of human and animal classification in which Africans—already slave labor in the New World—always ended up at the bottom of the chart.

But, being at root ideological, racism is also itself a kind of knowledge. And as a number of commentators have observed, an important part of its work is to make the world intelligible. The tendency and power of race, David Goldberg reminds us, is "to fix social subjects in place and time."[16] This was a power aptly suited to the swirling changes of an expansionist Europe. Similarly, modern racism would be codified and mature in the period of democratic revolutions that swept the Atlantic world in the late eighteenth and early nineteenth centuries.[17] Race made sense of worlds that, in the midst of anxious change, were otherwise opaque, unpredictable, and inchoate. In time race could "cover over the increasing anonymity of mass social relations in the modern world."[18]

But if the project of modernity begins by valorizing rationality, it ends with a thoroughgoing "rationalization" of systems of human organization, human labor, and all other manner of human social relations. Rationality and rationalization constitute power, the power to dominate. The twofold domination of the natural world and of the self are central themes of modernity from its earliest moments in the sixteenth century to debates over the wisdom of genetically engineering new plant, animal, or even human life at the turn of the twenty-first century.[19] And as that debate suggests, an essential first step on that path was that a secular worldview had gained primacy in everyday affairs. Clearly, the modern intellect and modern temperament resulted in much that was progressive and improving in the human condition, spiritually (religious toleration, for example) as well as materially (not only jet planes but lower infant mortality, for instance). But just as clearly modernity has had its dark side, which the catastrophe of the Nazi horror has led many thinkers to probe.[20]

I will not take on here the question of whether modernity inevitably led to totalitarian domination or even the many implications of the fact that the racist horror of the Holocaust is the disquieting centerpiece of twentieth-century history. Rather, our purpose is to explore the linkage between race and modernizing state systems. In ten lectures delivered at the Collège de France in the fall of

1976, Michel Foucault suggested that what modernizing states in general and the Nazi horror in particular have in common is the will to power over their internal populations, or what he calls "biopower." This power takes concrete form in politics with the regulation of the reproduction of the nation in all its multiple dimensions, thereby structurally embedding racist tendencies in every modern state. By the end of the nineteenth century, Foucault argues, a kind of state racism had emerged, rooted in the biopolitics of the state apparatus that had gradually accrued over the previous century. This biopolitics was rooted in the modern state's concern with policing the biological fitness of its population. Thus health and disease, fertility and declining birth rates, progress and degeneracy formed the binaries of a new racialized discourse, one in which the state sought to defend society against its own inferior members.[21] Inchoate and incomplete though they may be, Foucault's ideas might help us frame one of the crucial linkages between modernity and racism—in materialist as well as idealist terms.[22]

Aspects of Foucault's paradigm conform to the essential racial dynamic of American slavery, reminding us again of how essentially "modern" American slave plantations were.[23] Plantations were models of the modern virtues of rationality and rationalization. Many plantation ledgers display calculations of work routines and nurture as meticulously as those of Frederick Taylor, whose codicils of scientific management of industrial workers in the early twentieth century are taken by many analysts as markers of modern rationalization. Planters gave intense attention to processes that disciplined and normalized a bounded population, some of which clearly resemble those Foucault attributes to the modern state. There were careful records and statistical analyses of work processes, cold calculations of the efficient application of discipline, and detailed attention to the births, deaths, morbidity, fecundity, and natal care that determined the reproduction of the slave population and thus the plantation's profits.[24] In some cases such calculations led to the decision that it was cheaper to work a slave to death and buy new replacements from Africa than to provide the nutrition and care that would promote biological reproduction of the labor force. That this was not just a matter of the morality of individual planters but was rooted in the social environment and political economy of New World slavery as such is suggested by the novelty of biological reproduction of North American slave labor forces: only the slave population in Britain's North American colonies and the nineteenth-century United States managed consistently to reproduce itself.[25] Slavery in the Americas was nothing if not an example of biopower—the management of lives so that, in Foucault's cryptic summary, the privileged would be *made to live* while the unvalued would be *allowed to die* ("pouvoir de 'faire' vivre et de 'laisser' mourir").[26]

After slavery was abolished in the nineteenth century the planters' exercise of biopower was to some extent assumed by state systems. While contemporary states rely largely on the market to move masses of labor from places of labor surplus to places of labor shortage, some nineteenth-century states linked to plantation economies mobilized such movements directly. Shortly after slavery ended, hundreds of thousands of East Indians, Chinese, and free African laborers were relocated under indentured contracts from the Eastern Hemisphere to plantations and mines in the Americas. The arrangements for these bound laborers replicated many of the features of the earlier slave trade; a fact not lost on many contemporary observers.[27] The planters' preference for young males (often mere boys) who would be immediately available as field laborers upset the gender balance much as in the early years of the Atlantic slave trade. A major difference, however, was that the simple replacement of the labor force with new recruits was never supplanted by a policy of encouraging biological reproduction, as was the case in some slave systems.

The centrality of reproduction to the long-term viability of plantation systems in the Americas suggests why the disciplining of black women's bodies and sexuality loomed so large in the discourse and practice of American slavery. Racial and labor regimes were mutually dependent. With bound labor gradually becoming the exclusive burden of blacks, blackness became increasingly associated with slavery.[28] Consequently, the produce of black women's bodies was crucial to sustaining the produce of the fields, especially after the legal overseas slave trade was ended in 1807. These institutional structures in turn shaped the ideological and affective features of the racial system that emerged. For example, interracial sex might produce offspring whose status had to be resolved so as not to confound the racial rationale for slavery. Consequently, sexual reproduction by black men and white women—which was accepted with a fair degree of equanimity in the seventeenth century—acquired a different significance and came to be treated differently in law from that between white men and black women. First, in contrast with later decades, interracial sexual relations in the seventeenth century seem to have become a public problem only when children were the result. Second, in a social order in which the relations among whites were increasingly dependent on limiting servile labor to blacks only, the status of interracial offspring was more than a mere matter of sexual competition. Since children inherited the condition of their mothers, the offspring of a white male and a black female slave remained the property of the mother's owner, while the children of a white woman and a black male slave were legally free. Thus this fundamental asymmetry in gender and racial relations—later taken for granted as somehow "natural" and psychologically innate—actually evolved at a specific historical conjuncture.[29]

By focusing our attention on the link between reproduction and racial systems, therefore, Foucault encourages us to examine one of the historical and structural links between racial systems of very different eras as well as one of the ways in which history is gendered.[30] Racialized social systems and racial discourse have been animated by the mutual interaction of reproduction with labor and civil status from the beginnings of the slave era until the present day, when the image of black women as idle workers but active reproducers has shaped so much of the political discourse and politics of the late twentieth century.[31] In the first instance, reproduction was controlled and added to the planter's wealth; in the latter, reproduction is uncontrolled and ostensibly depletes the state's disbursements. In the first instance, the woman's sexuality is feared but secretly procured; in the second, it is feared and maligned. "She's a damn good breeder" takes on very different meanings in the two eras, not the least of which is that in the first a slave woman had an outside chance of receiving prenatal care from an enlightened, self-interested planter.

The relevance of all this for understanding the work that race does is that it illuminates some of the ideas that thread through contemporary racial discourse, as well as how ideas, images, and discourse can be rooted in structural, historical realities. For while it is true that race can be an empty vessel waiting to be filled with historically specific stuff, it is also sedimented with associations encrusted from earlier struggles. With these historical accretions our political discourse has become so thoroughly saturated with racialized references that phrases become "enriched" with hidden meanings, and words become double entendres that resonate differently among different racial communities. Thus can the infamous Willie Horton commercial of George Bush's 1992 presidential campaign persuade some that it is simply about preserving law and order, while for many others it is saturated with a discourse about the black-beast-rapist-on-the-loose used a century earlier to justify lynching. It is very likely that a similarly historically sedimented racialized image of uncontrolled reproduction, illicit sexuality, and status inconsistency saturates the infamous epithet "welfare queen."

Foucault's central idea, however, is the link between modern racism and the emergence of the modern state. With an eye on the rationalizing racial project of the Third Reich, Foucault generalizes its underlying premise to all modern state systems. By the early twentieth century it is the state that monopolizes biopower, a power constituted by knowledge and administrative control, a power by which life and lives are managed. In the name of progress and survival the state has the potential to promote and sanitize decisions of life and death, of morbidity and reproduction of the species. We shall return to this premise when we examine certain aspects of the transition to the Fordist and post-Fordist racial regimes, but before doing so it might be helpful to trace the complex relations between race and the nation-state from a longer-term perspective.

## RACE, NATIONALITY,
## AND NATIONAL FORMATION

As Columbus completed preparations for sailing off to the yet-to-be-discovered (by Europeans) New World, he penned a message to Ferdinand and Isabella congratulating them in passing on the recent military defeat of the Moors and the expulsion of the Jews. With the defeat of the Moors they reclaimed—and in reality constituted for the first time—a Spanish nation; with the purge of the Jews they ostensibly made it culturally one as well. With this message, therefore, Columbus linked race, temporally and materially, not only with one of the constitutive projects of modernity—the making of the nation—but also with his own imminent voyages of discovery and colonization. Thus the project of nation-building, the onset of imperial expansion, and a campaign of racial exclusion appear to be not only simultaneous but interrelated.

It might be argued, of course, that such an interpretation is anachronistic, because the Jewish expulsion was motivated by religion rather than by race and early modern Spain was by no means a prototypical nation-state. But 1492 can be taken as a protean moment in the evolution of race and nation that would in due course give them their modern forms; it would be equally anachronistic to expect such phenomena to be fully formed at birth. As J. H. Elliott, an eminent historian of imperial Spain, has put it: "The conquest of Grenada and the expulsion of the Jews had laid the foundations for a unitary state in the only sense in which that was possible in the circumstances of the late fifteenth century."[32] Indeed, purity of faith, Elliott notes, did the work of nationalism in this moment of Spanish national integration. One might add that in that same moment racism also took its only viable form: initially religion did the work of race; later race would work through religion. Within a very short time, therefore, as the Inquisition targeted the converted Jews of Castile, purity of faith was transmuted into "purity of blood." It was no longer religious beliefs but biological descent that determined one's claim to membership in the nation.[33] Unsurprisingly, the "racial" implications of purity of blood were clearest and manifested earliest in that hothouse of racial formation, the Americas, where African and Indian mestizo populations needed to be controlled and excluded from just claims on the state and economy.[34]

It seems hardly coincidental that modern nation-states evolved in the same era as racialized labor systems. The making of the modern nation-state, the fashioning of national consciousness, the fostering of racialized labor systems in the Americas, and the fashioning of racial identities were roughly contemporaneous and interrelated. Conceptually and materially nation-states in the modern sense of the term were born of sixteenth-century exploration and colonization. The thrust outward across the Atlantic and subsequently to the East required new forms of resource mobilization—to launch ships of exploration, to put armies in the field, to mobilize and transport thousands of slave laborers. Such mobilizations both required and prompted national formations of a more modern form.

But the structural link between race and nation was complemented by linkages that were more sociocultural and psychic, of which Spain's expulsion of Jews and Moors was emblematic. "As *concepts*," David Goldberg reminds us, "race and nation are largely empty receptacles through and in the names of which population groups may be invented, interpreted, and imagined as communities or societies."[35] Thus racial and national identities have been intertwined and mutually imbricated throughout the modern era. Complex and multivalent, their affective and effective entanglement has endured to the present day.

Modern national identity would build on the emergence of a new consciousness, Benedict Anderson suggests; one that enabled ordinary people to imagine themselves linked to a secular national community rather than to a sacred, hierarchical one.[36] Its institutional embodiment is to be found in printed books and newspapers as much as on sailing ships.

But it might be argued as well that nation-states call forth nationalism as a condition of their being and survival.[37] For that nationalism to be effective it must present itself as rooted in an immemorial past, as arising out of an (oftentimes) mystical peoplehood that is merely made manifest, is—in the double meanings of the word—*realized* by the creation of the nation-state. In other words, the authority for the nation-state preexists the bounded, sovereign entity that is brought into being. For this reason the icons, stories, myths, heroes and heroines—in effect much of what we group under the rubric of its cultural expression—comes to personify the nation's coming into being in the primordial past, but is crucial to sustaining it in the present. This is one reason there are fights over how history is taught, and over *what* history is taught—that is, what is the canon. Indeed, every revolutionary challenge to an existing order must take on the ideological task of rewriting the founding myths, must create new icons, new representations of the national entity. And by the same token, every fight over how the nation is to be defined is also a fight over its cultural representation.[38]

Or, at least this is true with the modern nation-state. Benedict Anderson suggests that one of the key differences between the premodern and the modern nation lies in the fact that the former is organized and conceptualized in vertical terms—both the power of the ruler and the ties that bind the individual to the nation radiate outward from the king or queen; while the latter is visualized in horizontal terms—power (and sovereignty) spread out evenly over a bounded territory, with individuals linked to it and to one another not as the subjects of a crown but as citizens, as members of a body politic.[39]

But what's the substance of this belonging? What content fills that abstract sense that individual A is a compatriot of individual B? Or, in Ernest Renan's famous late-nineteenth-century query: What is/makes a nation? By Renan's time, of course, the answer had been supplied, or at least had evolved. Nationals were linked by a common culture. They could trace their genealogies through language families. (And these linguistic groupings were and still are conceptualized as families, like the branches on a family tree, with geneticlike nodes in which one linguistic pattern begets another.) Consequently language—the cultural building block of nationality—could be and was easily assimilated to define racial belonging and to ordain racial boundaries. Thus the notion of an Aryan race begins its career as *a linguistic affinity*. Subsequently, this and other linguistic groupings (the Germanic peoples and the Anglo-Saxons, for example) are invoked to trace and define national lineages. Only later do they acquire racial meanings. Through this legerdemain, linguistic roots imply a racial destiny. Racial destiny comes to justify subordination and rule over other, less favored "races."[40]

A somewhat similar map and trajectory can be traced through religion, it being a cultural as well as (or perhaps more than) a spiritual concept. To say that one was a Christian in the sixteenth- and seventeenth-century Atlantic world was to invoke not just a set of religious beliefs but a script for living: acceptable behaviors, social values, sexual and familial relations—even table manners. In fact, for a brief moment in the seventeenth century, the line between slavery and freedom was first drawn between the heathen and the Christian.[41]

As cultural elements, then, language and religion not only signify or mark belonging; they are the media and processes through which one is made to belong. National cultures don't simply exist; they have to be made. And every new nation-in-the-making takes on a national project of cultural reformation. Britain did it during Cromwell's reign, France after the French Revolution, followed by America, China, and so forth. How one dressed, ate, worshipped, or enjoyed leisure time were all fair game for cultural reconstruction.[42]

It is from this phenomenon, perhaps, that Anderson draws his distinction between nationalism as being open to assimilating the outsider and racism as not. Perhaps. But closer examination suggests that the differences between racism and nationalism are not so simple or stark.[43] For example, the very process of incorporating the alien into citizenship is designated—in several languages—as "naturalization." The idea of literally being made "natural" by a civic ritual is itself intriguing. But its significance for our purposes here is its passing similarity to rituals of purification and inclusion in racial systems. Thus in medieval Spain the Jew could convert to Catholicism and thus escape, for a while, the burdens of the discrimination against Jews; in fact many converted Jews came to hold high civil posts in the Spanish bureaucracy. Later, however, this ceased to be possible as the Inquisition pursued a mythic purity of blood. Then the very ambiguity of the *converso* identity, born Jewish but acting Catholic, raised suspicion and fears of corruption of the faith from within. Though couched in religious discourse these are immemorial, archetypal racial fears. Eventually they prompted repression and expulsion of Jews altogether.[44] Thus the passage from culture (religion) to biology (purity of blood) was not a difficult one.

In the Americas one finds similar tensions and debates around the treatment of mulattos and mixed-blood peoples in the Caribbean and Latin America. At times and under certain circumstances, they came to occupy a social status not unlike the Jewish and Muslim converts. They were not classifed with blacks but as a separate caste, and they filled the interstitial jobs—and some of high status—that American frontier societies with small white settler populations required. In the British West Indies there were legal procedures—if one could pay for them—for having oneself actually declared white by an act of the legislature. In Jamaica in the 1830s the white planters hoped that the brown population could be assimilated to the white side of the racial divide so that they would form a protective bulwark against the soon-to-be-emancipated black slave majority.[45] Usually such positions of privilege were preserved for the mulattos and the near-whites, but there were many instances of what the Brazilians called "money lightening the skin," in which wealthy but obviously black people were recognized as whites. And, of course, closer to our own times, is the case of South Africa during the apartheid era: in order to reconcile apartheid laws with its ambitions for fostering international trade, the state granted the status of "honorary whites" to Japanese businessmen—something no Asian born in South Africa could hope to achieve.

This tension over assimilation-absorption, expulsion-extermination would resonate throughout the history of American racism, and with many different racialized groups (Indians, Asians, Mexicans, as well as blacks). In the history of race in the Americas, one finds racial categories varying over time and space. Indeed, there has never been a singular definition of who was and who was not white that stretches across the entire modern era. Indeed, the determination of racial identity was a constitutive part of the process of national formation.

The process is perhaps most obvious in the United States, which not only fought a civil war over slavery but consolidated its national identity in complex relation to the racial composition of its inhabitants. During the two decades before the Civil War, thousands of Irish and German immigrants landed on its shores and settled its cities and hinterland. Hector St. John de Crevecoeur's question of who and what is an American—which prefigured Renan's formulation—was posed again and again as issues of political alignment, labor, and consumption were debated. In those debates, whether framed by congressional arguments over slavery or by minstrel shows, class and national identities were, in Stuart Hall's words, "lived" and "fought through" the modality of race.[46] In the course of that debate European immigrants would claim a "whiteness" defined in part against the "blackness" of African-American slaves.

Other nations in the American hemisphere—at similarly critical moments of national formation and consolidation—found it useful to "play the race card." Conservative Cubans, frightened by the radical implications of their own revolution in 1898 and determined to claim a share of modernity urged discursive and practical policies to ensure a "white" future.[47] In late-nineteenth- and early-twentieth-century Brazil "whitening" took the form of inviting in white European immigrants to dilute its huge black majorities.[48] Ironically, in North America the compatriots of some of the "whites" Brazil was recruiting— Italians and Japanese—were finding their own claims to that status put in question.[49] These examples can be multiplied in many other locales—though admittedly with different inflections and historical specificities (Australia being one that particularly comes to mind).

**Perhaps a concrete case study**—that of Mexican Americans in the Southwest—will make clearer how often the boundaries between race and nation are ambiguous, mutually constituting, and clearly mediated by class forces and factors, namely the modernizing political economy of the late nineteenth and early twentieth centuries.

Unlike any other group racialized in America, except

the Indians, the Mexican-American experience is rooted in military conquest and colonization. Indeed, military conquest created the physical and conceptual space in which the very category "Mexican American" took form. In their history in the Southwest, especially in Texas, one can follow a gradual, relatively transparent process in which these conquered Mexicans became racialized.

Despite the ostensible protections negotiated in the peace treaty with Mexico, Mexican landholders in the Southwest were generally dispossessed of their land. There were exceptions to this development, however, particularly in the ranching areas of south Texas. The Anglo newcomers, finding that they could not simply supplant the ruling Mexican elites there, sought to forge economic and social alliances with them instead, in some cases even to merge into the indigenous elite, or to place themselves on top of the existing Mexican hierarchy. Intermarriage in particular offered the relatively impoverished Anglos access to land and power. It was in this sense, David Montejano argues, that "the social bases for postwar governance rested on the class character of the Mexican settlements."[50]

There were, however, other methods of achieving the equivalent of kinship, or at least fictive kinship bonds short of actual marriage contracts. Political and economic alliances could be secured through the sponsorship of baptisms or confirmations. With these rituals the sponsors became *compadres* and *comadres* of the Anglos they hosted. For lower-status ranchero families who could not aspire to match their daughters with the Anglo elite, the *compradrazgo* ritual provided an alternative way of allying their families with the new entrepreneurial and political upper class. Anglo merchants and lawyers seized upon this "quasi-religious institution" in order to secure recognition, status, and protection. Meanwhile "the wealth and power of the landed elite were generally left undisturbed," with these various forms of social intercourse acting to bind the old and the new elites together.[51]

This arrangement between Anglos and Mexicans was inherently unstable and temporary, however. The new Anglo elites were mostly merchants and lawyers bent on transforming the political economy of the Southwest through increased trade and commercialization. They initiated a process that would be completed by other Anglos who were less inclined to adopt Mexican culture or political alliances with Mexicans. The latter group created a market in land and with it a new basis for class relations, all of which led to the demise of the old Mexican elite. By 1900 they were gone.[52]

The racialization of Mexicans proceeded in tandem with these political-economic transformations. A Mexican American's "race" depended on a delicate class geography and temporality: quite simply, the Mexican elites were more likely to be treated white in the ranching areas in the earlier period than in the commercial farming areas in the late nineteenth and early twentieth centuries. As an area moved through successive class orders—ranching, commercial farming, and urban-industrial—the nature of race relations changed. As Montejano succinctly puts it: "Mexicans were more of a race in one place and less of a race in another." To which we might add, they were more of a race at one *time* and less in another. For by the early twentieth century, whatever his wealth or cultural pretensions, a Mexican in Texas was "simply a Mexican."[53]

In many ways the experience of Mexicans in south Texas was unique, different even from that of other Mexicanos in Colorado and California. Indeed, the social geography of race was very different just a few hundred miles to the north in central Texas, a region Neil Foley calls an "ethnoracial middle ground."[54]

In south central Texas, where the commercialization and proletarianization of farm labor proceeded faster, white farm owners replaced white and black sharecroppers with Mexicans, whom they considered more docile. In a race-class dynamic similar to that evolving in south Texas, Mexicans were treated as nonwhite, even though legally defined as white for some purposes. Thus even though miscegenation laws forbade marriages between blacks and whites, unions between African Americans and Mexicans were not prosecuted.[55]

This tripartite racial terrain encouraged some middle-class Mexican Americans to distance themselves not only from blacks but also from working-class Mexicans, especially immigrants. Thus LULAC (League of United

Latin American Citizens), founded by Mexican-American veterans in 1929, embraced assimilation and restricted its membership to English-speaking U.S. citizens. A LULAC member who married "a Negress" was expelled. In El Paso the group fought the U.S. Census Bureau's decision to reclassify them as "Mexican" rather than "white."[56]

These reactionary responses reveal the tripartite link between race, political economy, and nationality. A claim to "whiteness"—originally established by the link to a Mexican nation—was gradually effaced as Mexican settlers were increasingly linked to lower-class labor. The labor status in south central Texas was not mediated by the existence of a landed elite, as in the South. As conquered elites, Mexican Americans claimed a national heritage that made them honorary whites; but as immigrant labor they were relegated to a status—both practically and, increasingly, legally—of *not* white.

Critical features of the Mexican-American experience were shared with other racial groups in the United States. Every racial group was incorporated into the nation through the processes either of expropriating its land or exploiting its labor. In the course of that essentially political-economic process, they were racialized, that is, made into races. Also similar to the Mexican-American experience, nationality claims mediated or inflected the meaning of race for many of these groups, producing some of the contrastive features of their life and destiny in America.

For many of these groups that common process of racialized incorporation was shaped—and sometimes moderated—by their capacity to claim an alternative nationality. Early on, Indians were defined—and from time to time were actually treated—as nations within the nation. Perhaps this treatment reflected the anachronism of the very different earlier resonances of race and nation continuing in the jurisprudence and law of a later period. In any case, it was a common disposition in the era of America's geographical expansion. For example, black residents in some of the territories acquired from France and Spain (Louisiana and parts of Alabama and Florida) could lay claim to treaty rights, which gave them a different civil status from other black Americans.[57] As already noted, Mexicans were defined as nationals by the terms of the Treaty of Guadalupe Hidalgo, which gave them some limited defense against land seizures. At various times Asian groups have made similar claims, as in the case of the Japanese government's successful intervention to prevent San Francisco from segregating its compatriots in public schools in 1906.

Of course, the effectiveness and resonance of such claims depended very much on the relative power relation of such nations in the international order—as in the case of Japan, fresh from its triumph over Russia. The treaty rights extended to blacks of French and Spanish origins notwithstanding, to this day most African Americans have lacked such claims to extranational connection and protection. Being unable to lay claim to any given African nation produces a "nationlessness" that may explain the contrary phenomenon wherein intense and persistent Black Nationalist sentiments compete with equally intense claims to an American patrimony.

Throughout the modern era, therefore, race, culture, and nation have articulated in different ways at different historical moments. Both race and nation were progeny of European expansion and the evolution of modern political economies. Both were instrumental in forging boundaries as older markers of identity and difference weakened or dissolved, as a world evolved for which they were incapable of accounting. At various points in history race and nation have done similar work and have often been mutually imbricated. These concepts have made seemingly intelligible an unfolding order of things, have often been the balm for the socially dangerous anxieties of people facing a rapidly changing social environment, a radically new *habitus.*

Thus a linkage evident in embryonic form in the Spanish expulsion of Jews and Moors in the sixteenth century has been shaping national formations, citizenship, and racial politics ever since. That there should have been this long and complex interplay between race and nation in the modern world is very suggestive for how we might understand the work of race at the end of the twentieth century. For how is this relationship transfigured in the world we currently inhabit, where racial regimes and nation-states are undergoing yet another season of rapid transformation? Those changes have suggested to some that "the end of racism" is at hand. Perhaps. But before we unilaterally disarm the antiracist forces, we should reflect on the complex history of race, trace its amazing capacity for reproducing itself on radically different social bodies throughout the modern era.

# 2

# Race and Culture
# in a Consumer Society

T hus far I have attempted to demonstrate the historically contingent nature of race and racism in general, and in particular their intimate articulation with major processes that defined the development of the modern world. Prominent among those processes was the development of the modern nation-state and nationalism. All these processes were grounded in the first instance, however, in the political-economic transformations of modernity. Underpinning those developments, I along with many other scholars would insist, were the slave trade and slavery in the Atlantic world. Political, cultural, and social life on both sides of the Atlantic was firmly rooted in those economic institutions and developments. For example, the coffeehouses of seventeenth-century London, celebrated by Jürgen Habermas as sites for the formation of the bourgeois democratic public sphere, were also sites for making deals to insure slave cargoes traversing the Atlantic from Africa to the Americas; Lloyds of London and Barclays Bank originated in such sites. Thus were the values and practices of everyday life (drinking a cup of coffee) invisibly linked to larger structures and processes.[1]

Indeed, long after slavery's abolition in the Americas, the structures it had put in place (the plantation system and global labor recruitment) and the goods it had produced (sugar, coffee, cotton, tobacco) continued to shape that world, in the large, structural aspects of existence as in the small corners of everyday life. Many of the social aftereffects of slavery, and more importantly of the labor systems that replaced it, stretched well into the twentieth century, and indeed some continue to shape our social environment today. But in much of the former Atlantic system the racial terrain was entering a process of profound transformation even as the last American slave systems—in Cuba and Brazil—were being dismantled.

As Du Bois observed in 1903, the problem of the twentieth century would be race relations, but as he came to appreciate scarcely two decades later, those relations would not take the same form as racial phenomena of the previous century. The changes in the meanings of race and racism in the twentieth century—already fully evident by the end of its second decade—were profoundly linked to the relative subordination of productive relations to consumption. This transformation in racial regime was interpellated with the broader cultural developments that transformed Western industrial nations into consumer societies. Such developments were especially evident in America, where increasingly both the formation of the racial system and resistance to it moved out of workshops and into spaces of consumption—into houses, stores, movies, and sport.[2]

Having said so much, I must immediately enter a caveat. As Adam Smith recognized long ago, production and consumption are dialectically related: there can be no production without a consumer, and there is nothing to consume if there is no production. By the same token, any prospective consumer needs income—in most cases, that is, excluding theft—in order to consume, which necessarily raises the question of employment and one's relation to the productive side of life.

The fact remains, however, that African Americans who began the century facing the problem of being a subordinated but essential part of the southern agricultural labor force and an underpaid, emerging segment of northern industrial labor, have finished the century facing a statistically greater chance than whites of being unemployed or never-employed. Despite its unfortunate title, this was the primary thesis, I believe, of William Julius Wilson's study, *The Declining Significance of Race,* more than two decades ago.[3] Race had not declined in significance, but it had radically shifted the terrain on which it was most socially relevant.

Although the substance and timing of this story get more complicated when we include other racialized groups and other parts of the world (colonialism complicates the picture for Europe and much of the Southern Hemisphere, for example), there is reason to think that the basic trajectory is much the same: a labor market increasingly segmented into three broad categories—one with relatively stable professional or skilled service jobs, one with increasingly shrinking industrial positions monopolized all the more tenaciously by a white labor aristocracy, and one defined by a plethora of poorly paid and decidedly unsteady light-manufacturing and unskilled service jobs. Ironically, some of the latter at times verge on approximating slave labor occupations of a bygone era—a condition found not only in East Asian sweatshops but in East Los Angeles as well. To say that the terrain of racial formation has shifted more from relations of production to those of consumption, therefore, is by no means a claim that the economy (in the traditional sense) no longer plays a role in shaping the meaning of race. The economy's role, however, is now more indirect and mediated through a consumer society. Here I want to sketch the history of that change and to suggest something about its implications for understanding race and racism in our present and future.

## The Fordist Regime

The Fordist era takes its name from the industrial regime identified with Henry Ford, which is not to suggest either that Ford was responsible for it or embodied all its features or characteristics. It was, first of all, a regime involving a fundamental reorganization of both work processes and the political-economic assumptions of capitalism. These changes in political-economic assumptions and productive relations led in turn to major changes in consumption, both qualitative and quantitative, and in the powers and role of the state in everyday life.[4] Collectively these developments altered the ground on which racism took shape, as well as the basis for resistance to it.

It is well known that Henry Ford's minute division of labor on his automotive assembly line permitted fantastically greater quantities of goods to be produced at cheaper prices. Equally important to the success of that system, however, was his explicit attention to the fact that much greater consumption by the working class was a necessary precondition for sustained—or indeed ever-increasing—production. Ford recognized, as did many others, that the worker was a consumer as well as a producer; and in order for the system as a whole to be viable, workers must have wages adequate to buy the products they produced. Mass production required mass consumption. And, over time, the entire national economy came to depend on people's consuming not just what they needed, but *more* than they needed, with need itself being redefined by modern psychologically informed advertising.[5]

Enabling that level of consumption required not just higher wages (the immediate growth of which was slight) but the ready availability of credit and the willingness to use it. Thus the 1920s witnessed a veritable explosion in installment debt as loans for cars, household appliances, and other durable goods mushroomed. Mass consumption also meant mass debt. (Although Ford gave his name to this system, he was in truth not its most thoroughgoing advocate or thinker; he strongly opposed installment debt, for example.) The change was not simply quantitative, however; increasingly debt was provided through impersonal, anonymous debt servers rather than via actual merchants in face-to-face encounters. Indeed, automobile companies led the way in fashioning new institutional mechanisms for supplying credit to a greatly expanded public.[6]

The change in creditor-debtor relations is emblematic of the fact that the Fordist political economy did not simply set in motion an interrelated mix of changes in how labor and laborers were allocated to productive processes; it also transformed the nature and meaning of consumption and how the polity was constituted. More fundamentally, it changed people's *habitus,* that is, their lived environment, the material basis for their thought, the ground on which their fundamental relations with other people took form. In short, the relations between people, their goods, and their very sense of self—their everyday—were profoundly reshaped. Within a generation—and across a surprisingly broad social spectrum—the expectation, if not the fact, of owning a car, a radio, household appliances, and so on became prevalent and plausible, and thus changed people's perceptual if not immediately their material environment. Although these changes were uneven across race, class, and region, they were inexorable.

To say inexorable is not to say inevitable or automatic. Since the 1930s the basic axiom of all government economic policy has been to assure a "consuming public," one large enough and sufficiently motivated to sustain ever-increasing production through consumer spending. Historian Meg Jacobs has shown how a group of liberal businessmen (most prominently Boston's own Edward Filene—known for his gigantic retail store), progressive politicians (like Senator Robert F. Wagner of New York, author of the National Labor Relations Act of 1935), and reformist social scientists (like Leon Keyserling, a New Deal adviser and member of the first Council of Economic Advisers) fostered an economic policy analysis emphasizing the need for government intervention to create and sustain purchasing power.[7]

The slowness with which the South (and thus blacks, who were still overwhelmingly resident in the South) experienced these transformations in consumption points up the important and growing role of the state in shaping the everyday life of its citizens and the fact that these changes were politically contested. It was during the long tenure of Franklin Roosevelt that Fordist advocates like Edward Filene and Leon Keyserling gained access to the power of the state and used it—unevenly and haltingly to be sure—to extend the consumer society nationally. It was the New Deal state that brought rural electrification to the rural South. New Deal agricultural policies sped up the process by which blacks were pushed out of southern agriculture altogether, setting up the social basis—that is, an urbanized proletariat—for future challenges to the racial system of that region.

Although state interventions of this kind are part of what characterizes liberal Democratic political regimes, what is most striking from a long-term perspective is their pervasiveness. While specific policies and practices may differ, the idea that the government is implicated in this chain of production-consumption has endured through presidential administrations of varying political complexions. You may remember President George Bush visiting a supermarket in 1992 and buying a pair of socks in a vain effort to regenerate the consumer confidence and spending that might save his presidency. Humorous as the image might be of Bush at the checkout counter, trying to save the economy with his single pair of socks, it is emblematic of the enduring, complex interconnections between consumption, the economy, and the state that emerged in the interwar period.

The close tabs that investors and government policymakers now keep on those key economic indicators—durable-goods orders and new housing starts—is so routine a part of our world that it may be difficult to imagine another era. But it was during the Great Depression that the federal government established the Home Owners' Loan Corporation to save homeowners from foreclosure by extending long-term, low-interest mortgages to urban homeowners.[8] Other housing legislation and institutions—not only here but in other industrial democracies—laid the basis for those closely watched economic indicators that we are still watching in our morning papers. Indeed, it could be argued that the individual choice of buying and furnishing a house stands at the nexus of the entire modern economic complex.

But the implications of this nexus are more than economic. Lizabeth Cohen has described how, during the

New Deal, white ethnic workers turned to the national state for the first time to solve everyday problems and deliver the American dream.[9] In the postwar era housing would loom larger still among those entitlements, involving both direct assistance with purchases and invisible subsidies like tax deductions.

The story I have just described, of course, can be delivered with a different inflection; it is part of the litany, sometimes jeremiad, of conservative political commentators on what went wrong with America and the need to crush the New Deal state. But the fact that these transformations developed over a broad range of polities and political ideologies—in this country and in Europe—suggests a historical development on a scale that renders such complaints merely nostalgic. Transformed relations of the state with capital, labor, and consumption in the Fordist era provided the basis for consolidation of a multinational capitalist world system.

The ownership of capitalist enterprises tended to be corporate and publicly traded rather than entrepreneurial, and their economic fates dominated the economic fates of entire communities and regions. Notwithstanding the ideological strictures of neoclassical economics, these new realities also called forth (and often with the "self-made" capitalist entrepreneur doing the calling) an unprecedented level of state intervention in the economy, not only as regulator of competition and conditions of trade but as the de facto banker of last resort.[10] At the na-

tional level, Keynesian economic policies sought to regu-
late or fine-tune the fit between production and consumption, and welfare policies sought to soften the social
impact of the business cycle. At the international level,
multinational agreements regulated the flow of goods,
services, and currencies. Such changes in both political-
economic regime and in lived experience—in *habitus*—
raises the question of what kind of racial regime they
might in turn give rise to.

## RACE IN A FORDIST ECONOMY

We can perhaps make clearer the changes in racial regime
contingent on the new Fordist era political economy by
drawing out the contrast with the essential features of the
system that preceded it. Although I have been treating this
pre-Fordist era as one, there are obviously a lot of differences between the period of slavery and the one immediately following. Nonetheless, slavery and the postemancipation era share some broadly similar modalities
of racial relations, not least of which is that under both
systems, blacks came closer perhaps than they ever would
again to full employment. As Jesse Jackson is reported to
have said (with a sly smile one imagines): "During slavery,
*everybody* had a job." With some justice, one might say
the same about the postemancipation era.

From the early nineteenth century to its final decades,
at which point most slave systems had been replaced by

postemancipation regimes of juridically free labor, the demand for cheap, docile labor continued apace. I use "docile" in this instance not to characterize the laborers but the conditions under which they labored. Wage labor, sharecropping, indentured contracts were all calibrated to limit freedom of movement and/or alternative employment, generally through legal constraints rather than whips— though whips would be wielded when laws were not up to the task. In those places in the Americas where former slaves could not be coerced back into the fields by economic means or state regulations or violence, the state sponsored or supported the importation of other racialized workers—usually from India or China and usually under some form of indenture or contract. All of which complicated the labor regime by introducing a plurality of races, and complicating as well the racial geography of and race relations within the hemisphere. (Such complications have only recently come under scrutiny in the United States, as we slowly realize that "race" is not a synonym for "black.") Indeed, the state played an increasingly aggressive and crucial role throughout this period, but, unlike in the twentieth century, it usually represented a much more distant force and a resource of last resort.

Thus both slave and postemancipation regimes were contingent on, even dependent on, keeping blacks and other racialized groups *physically* in their place—which, in the United States, was largely at work in the agricultural and extractive industries of the South and Southwest. Not

surprisingly, the forms that blacks' resistance to this regime took was to escape "their place." Slaves tried literal
escape; sharecroppers tried movement and migration. In
the United States, slaves lost themselves in southern and
northern cities; elsewhere they built great maroon colonies—in the mountainous or jungle interiors of Jamaica,
Surinam, and Brazil, or in the swamps of Alabama, Louisiana, and North Carolina. After emancipation—in the
Americas and in Africa—they organized their communities politically, economically, and socially. They joined
civil protests, religious movements, and labor movements. When all else failed, they migrated away—to the
American West, to the Caribbean, to Africa, to Europe,
but almost always to cities and towns.

None of these individual or small collective efforts to
escape "their place," however, would have an effect equal
in either quantitative or qualitative scale to that occa-
sioned by the changes in political economy I have just described. The Fordist political economy brought fundamental shifts in the very framework for race relations on a
vast geographic scale. The new mass-production, mass-
consumption regime's voracious appetite for labor produced mass black migrations at unprecedented levels in
the early twentieth century: from South to North in the
United States, from colony to metropole in the British
and French West Indies, from country to city in southern
and western Africa. In brief, millions of colored peoples
on four continents were quite literally pulled or pushed

out of "their place." This migration meant that for the first time in history the world's black population—from Cape Town to Detroit, from São Paulo to Dakar—would soon be predominately urban rather than predominantly rural. It followed as a consequence that in each location one finds some counterpart of the story we are so familiar with in the United States: the breakdown of the paternalistic modes of racial interaction that characterized both slavery and sharecropping; a greater integration of blacks into the national economy, and of black culture into national cultures; and, most important, the tendency for the state to take a greater direct role in the regulation of race relations.

There is irony, perhaps even a symbolic symmetry, in the fact that the man who gave his name to this era was also instrumental in recruiting African Americans into that new economy in the United States. Henry Ford was a segregationist and an anti-Semite, but he set out to hire blacks for his plants, working through the Urban League and prominent black ministers in Detroit. Outstripping all other automakers, Ford's aggressive recruitment garnered about half of all blacks working in the auto industry during the interwar period, peaking in the 1930s at 11 percent of the entire workforce at the infamous River Rouge plant.[11]

Given Henry Ford's demand that the recruits be "respectable" blacks, the black churches became, in effect, his employment agencies, screening their congregations for morally upright and reliable workers. A quid pro quo, of course, was that these ministers' own power in the black community was greatly enhanced. The significance of this development for our purposes, however, is that at an early date blacks became a not insignificant part of one of the core industries of the new economy.[12] Eventually these workers would lead the movement of blacks into labor unions, in particular into the United Auto Workers, a move that would have complicated consequences for black civil rights and liberation movements in the mid-twentieth century. Sea change though this development was, however, it was not around employment or unionization that the major racial conflicts of the following decades would take shape. Rather it was housing—a key item in the market basket of the new consumption regime—that became one of the key sites of racial conflict in that new economy.

Ten years after Ford's recruitment began, Detroit faced a growing problem of where to house its burgeoning population. As is often the case, what whites experienced as a problem was for blacks a crisis. The issue burst forth with particular force in the fall of 1925, when a black doctor, Henry Ossian Sweet, was charged with murder along with his wife, son, and several friends. Upon moving into a heretofore all-white neighborhood, Sweet and his family found themselves surrounded by a threatening mob. Having expected trouble the Sweets had come prepared, armed with several guns and ammunition. During the altercation someone in the house fired into the crowd, killing one member of the mob and wounding another. Unable to determine who actually fired the shot, the state brought murder charges against all the persons in the house. Clarence Darrow, retained by the NAACP to defend the Sweets, eventually secured an acquittal.[13]

The case became a cause célèbre in black communities nationally. On the face of it, the Sweets confronted the racial terrors of old—the lynch mob and hostile officers of the law. Thus the recent southern origins of many Detroit whites and the recent resurgence of the Ku Klux Klan in northern and southern cities were themes in much of the coverage in the black press.[14] But other, newer themes emerged in both public and private discourse around this trial that would resonate with the confrontations of the decades to come rather than with those of the century past.

In the *Sweet* case, blacks were being denied the right not only to a house—a physical space to live—but to an identity—as citizens in a polity, as persons in the process of social self-realization. Not only would these themes be woven through Darrow's masterful (and very long) summation for the defense; they would resonate in contemporary press coverage and in arguments and briefs of later years. Darrow's defense dwelled heavily on the evident class difference between the upwardly mobile Sweets—he, a Howard University M.D. who had received specialist training in Paris and Vienna; she, a lady of cultured manners and classical education—in contrast with the vulgar manners of the white mob and onlookers. Similarly, NAACP press briefings would emphasize the necessity for blacks of culture and class mobility to find housing outside the burgeoning ghettos created by the Great Migration.[15]

Years later, in a 1947 memorandum to President Truman, Thurgood Marshall would sound similar themes though somewhat differently articulated. Marshall's memo protested rules and procedures of federal agencies like the Federal Housing Administration, which actually supported segregated housing despite an overall government policy ostensibly supporting integration. "Housing, in our society today," Marshall wrote, "is more than shelter. It includes the whole environment in which the home is maintained." Thus segregation frustrated the national policy "to provide for Americans a healthful home environment, both physically and psychologically."[16]

Increasingly then, a house and its neighborhood were among those items of consumption by which people constituted *who* they were. Consequently it became a site of racial contestation in the early twentieth century as the sheer possibility of actually owning a home became more and more available to middle- and working-class people— black and white. For the "not-yet-white" ethnics who were so often in the forefront of these violent protests, house and neighborhood were part of their portfolio of whiteness;[17] thus their articulation of their opposition to black neighbors in terms of a decline in property values.[18] For the black middle class, the grievance was often articulated as the unjust denial of their need to represent their material and cultural achievement; if their emergence was strangled stillborn in the ghettos, their very existence was in some sense at risk.[19]

Thomas Sugrue's work on the same city has shown how this complex mix of racial and cultural meanings continued into the postwar era: "homeownership," he writes, "was as much an identity as a financial investment." "Houses were symbolic extensions of the self, of the family."[20] Sugrue explicates that observation by revealing a process by which traditional values linking home with patrimony got linked in turn to the new values of the consumer society of the early twentieth century; homeownership became an outward sign of success, of probity (in more objective language, creditworthiness), and of having made it into the American middle class. By an inverse process, then, racial exclusion was conflated with the protection of these claims and parades under the rubric "property values."[21] The meaning of the "value" alluded to here can work only at a metadiscursive level. By that I mean that much like the contemporary stock market, property values might in fact decline when blacks like the Sweet family move into the neighborhood, but simply because their neighbors sell their homes at a loss, *expecting* values to decline. The expectation fulfills its own prophecy.

As Sugrue suggests, with this legerdemain began a

process whereby the racial geography of a city was mapped and with it a fragile white racial identity was sustained.[22] The facts that the "not-yet-white" ethnics were the most likely to resist housing integration violently, and that these became the heart of the politically conservative racial backlash from the late 1960s on, underscore this point.[23]

Often the conflict is discursively constructed so that its racist character is disguised. Racism colonizes other categories and concepts—like economic rationality and justice, and notions of value and entitlement. Black advancement gets linked to big government and otherwise relatively privileged whites (indeed privileged by that same government) come to claim the "little guy" role and march under the banner of populism. The political salience of this development can be readily seen in the political careers of George Wallace and Ronald Reagan in the United States, Margaret Thatcher and Jean-Marie Le Pen in Europe. In a kind of cosmic, ideological "bait and switch" the top dog becomes underdog.

Although production brought blacks to Detroit, then, it was around consumption that issues of race were most fervently and consistently joined. But consumption was not—perhaps never has been—simply a matter of buying and selling; it played powerfully on the formation of identity more generally and in these instances on racial identity in particular. Thus did housing, one of those closely watched indicators of economic health in a Fordist economy, also become a signifier of racial meaning.[24]

### RACE ON THE TERRAIN OF CULTURE

In a sense, then, housing serves as a bridge in this discussion, taking us from political economy to culture. I suggested earlier that culture has always borne a complex relation with race and racial phenomena—conceptually and practically. But in the period we are discussing now, that relationship intensifies—qualitatively and quantitatively —as culture itself becomes increasingly commodified.

This was, for example, a period during which sporting contests were organized and professionalized; and with that change, events and vicarious experiences were bought and sold like any other goods. Issues of racial association and access were raised that had not even been thought of, much less been relevant, before. Jack Johnson's or Joe Louis' victories over white competitors in the boxing ring or Jackie Robinson's on the baseball diamond could have broad social consequences—could, for example, affect how both blacks and whites thought of themselves and their relations to one another. This was possible, however, only on the precondition that the organization and consumption of such activities had taken on meanings for the general populace that were more than mere play.

Although the roots of many of the themes I will explore here lie in nineteenth-century cultural forms, the narrative of culture and race in the twentieth century has many more complex layers. Some of these might best be illustrated by boxing—a sport focused on two bodies rather than on a team, and on a singular moment, "the fight." As a consequence, perhaps, the fighters and the fight assume qualities much like texts; indeed, before TV they were most often experienced *through* texts and thus lend themselves to something like a textual analysis. Moreover, boxing is a sport that emerges into professional prominence roughly contemporaneous with the Fordist era.

Almost simultaneous with Ford's inauguration of the new machine age in Detroit, Jack Johnson convulsed white America by destroying "the White Hope," Jim Jeffries, appropriately enough on the Fourth of July 1910. Riots erupted in more than fifty cities (an outburst comparable in size to what followed Martin Luther King's assassination in 1968, when scores of cities went up in flames). On the face of it, it seems that the society literally acted out its racial hatred and angst—giving graphic illustration to Clifford Geertz's idea that what seems to be "only a game" in a given culture is often "more than a game."[25]

But then perhaps the story is not so simple as all that: a black man beats a white man; whites riot. Especially puzzling is the fact that this response to Johnson's *defense* of his title was very different from that to his having won the title in the first place. There had been little prefight coverage and no postfight violence when Johnson defeated the then champion Tommy Burns in Australia two years earlier. Although the distant site of the match undoubtedly played a role, Jill Dupont's examination of the discourse around the second fight has brought to the surface other, unexpected dimensions of the Johnson-Jeffries fight of 1910. In striking contrast with the John Henry legend of black muscle struggling against a machine, the metaphorical valence of this racial confrontation was reversed in the commentaries before and after the fight. The imagery woven around this fight identified the white Jeffries with a virile primitivity and the black Johnson with modernity. Jeffries was portrayed as coming out of nature and the wilderness: he was brute strength, a natural fighter. Johnson was of the city, a high, fast-living dandy. But despite this oblique reference back to minstrelsy, he was also portrayed as a scientific boxer, as clever, skillful, machinelike. In myriad ways, Dupont argues, Jeffries stood in at this moment of intense socioeconomic change for a simple and comforting past, while Johnson was the angst-ridden future. Indeed, in some subtle ways Jeffries was the solidity of production, while Johnson was a threatening over-consumption.[26]

Of course, the more complex symbolism that formed around Johnson the boxer was counterbalanced by other, more traditional racial imagery. But that duality should not distract attention from a pattern of representation in which a racial image is appropriated for nonracial (or should I say supraracial) ends. It was a duality that, as we shall see, continues well into the present era. So, for example, Joe Louis was at times portrayed in cartoons taken straight out of the minstrel songbook: slow-thinking, sleepy, shuffling, and chicken-eating. By the 1940s, however, Joe Louis was embraced as an all-American hero—especially after he enlisted in the army in 1942. As one sportswriter greeted the news of his enlistment: "We are all one in America now," in a commentary reflecting the extent to which Louis' persona and career had come to stand in for the nation as a whole in a moment of national peril.[27] A long and growing line of black sports heroes, from Jackie Robinson to Michael Jordan, would play out similar though changing dualities. And especially in this later case (Jordan), the nexus between production and consumption and race would be exposed in all of its complexity.

One other important new site of racial confrontation emerged on explicitly cultural terrain early in this century, one that reflects some of the complexity of the growing linkage between race, culture, and consumer society, and one that still has resonance for the racial problematic we are still trying to unravel. In 1915, the year Jack Johnson was defeated by the new "White Hope," Jess Willard, D. W. Griffith's *Birth of a Nation* opened to rave reviews and determined protests. The film was a cinematic rendition of Thomas Dixon's racist novel *The Clansman*. The brutal racism of Dixon's novel was softened at its edges, but both novel and film celebrated the redemption of the Old South from the alleged ravages of political domination by blacks and northern carpetbaggers during Reconstruction. Here I want to draw attention to some striking features in the reaction to the film that mark it as a departure in the representation of race and the resistance to it.[28]

Woodrow Wilson's famous response upon screening the film in the White House was: "It was like writing history with lightning."[29] In ways Wilson himself could not have imagined, his analogy speaks powerfully to what was indeed at stake, focusing attention on this medium's new-found power—one that, like lightning, can illuminate *and* do great harm. Lightning, an elemental, primitive force, is also associated with the modern—as in electricity, where it is tamed and harnessed to domestic ends.

It was a power that blacks, led by the recently formed National Association for the Advancement of Colored People (NAACP), quickly grasped, and they mounted protests from Los Angeles to New York to Boston in an effort to squash Griffith's film. As film historian Thomas Cripps has shown, however, this protest centered on efforts to censor the film in whole or in part, a move that even many of the NAACP leadership were ambivalent about and one that ultimately failed. Indeed, there is an uncomfortable irony in the fact that one of the laws that NAACP lawyers invoked to stop the film was the one prohibiting the showing of boxing films, which originated in the attempt to censor films of Jack Johnson's victory over Jim Jeffries.[30]

*The Birth of a Nation* opened a chapter in the struggle to control the image and imagery of blacks in the electronic age that continues to this day. Interestingly, the NAACP has been at the center both of these earlier efforts and of recent protests against the absence of black characters in prime-time television shows. The organization's program during the 1930s is usually identified with the campaign it mounted for federal lynching legislation, but at the same time the organization protested the stereotypes broadcast in the radio show *Amos 'n' Andy*. Here too the response was somewhat ambivalent; for reasons that Melvin Patrick Ely has detailed, the show was widely popular with blacks as well as with whites. Despite its direct links with the minstrel tradition in style and substance, the show was also a source of both technical innovation and complexity in its portrayals of black character. It was only after the Second World War that the campaign against it succeeded, and then perhaps less because of a unified black opposition (which never quite materialized) than because of the changing nature of TV sponsorship, which made commercial support for controversial shows risky.[31]

As George Lipsitz has shown, the link being forged between the consumption of goods and the consumption of entertainment was completed in 1950s television.[32] In yet another one of those sad ironies, therefore, the victory over *Amos 'n' Andy* came when—in the TV medium— black actors replaced whites wearing blackface. Indeed, even before the show was taken off the air, some sense of the change over the intervening years can be glimpsed from contrasting the scenes, first in Chicago's Washington Park, circa 1931, where Gosden and Correll were feted by a huge black audience led by the *Chicago Defender,* and then twenty years later, when their black successors were reviled and ignored.[33]

There are two larger points in this story for our purposes, however. First, blacks—out of "their place"—could and would choose to mobilize to protest the showing of racist films like *The Birth of a Nation* or radio shows like *Amos 'n' Andy,* something scarcely contemplated during the minstrel era of the nineteenth century. Second, they were not alone in recognizing the new social power involved in these media; at least some of those who sought to defend the racial status quo realized that power as well. In 1943, for example, the Board of Censors in Memphis, responding to race riots in Los Angeles and Detroit that year, resolved to ban any movie "in which an all negro cast appears or in which roles are depicted by negro actors or actresses not ordinarily performed by members of the colored race in real life."[34] Thus not only was the representation of history contested (as in *The Birth of a Nation*), but in this instance the possibility of even imagining an alternative future. Indeed, this proactive rather than reactive response—to create new imaginaries rather than react to old—characterizes part of today's struggles in this venue, as suggested by the recent NAACP-led protests against the absence of black characters in prime-time TV programming (rather than against the nature of their characterization).[35]

I am well aware that the story I have told thus far—of the growing linkages between the politics of race, the rise of a consumer society, and the growing commodification of culture—is one that relies heavily on selected vignettes, mere snapshots if you will from a epic drama. Other scholars are elaborating more-detailed narratives and fine-grained analyses of some of these phenomena. There is work, for example, going beyond the simplistic observation that the civil rights movement unfolded on TV, to look at the role of radio in the 1940s and other developments that literally mediated the relations among peoples and powers;[36] work also that interrogates the significance of the fact that the weapons of the weak in this case involved consumer boycotts and picketing of downtown merchants;[37] work that follows the racial confrontations that unfolded in the domain of culture and cultural reproduction, which entailed in turn intimate links with the evolving consumer society. All these issues and mediations have come to the fore with full force in the cultural, political, and economic life of the late twentieth century.

Here I hope to have put these later developments into that larger frame of historical reference, thus indexing some of their broader, enduring social implications. The fact that *Amos 'n' Andy* was among the very first national broadcasts on the new medium of radio in the late 1920s and then again on television in the 1950s forms a kind of symbolic bookend to the presence of blacks in American culture today, when in much of the rest of the world—and especially for people in the street—African-American sports and cultural figures constitute a kind of synecdoche for America.[38] It may be said that a similar bookend is formed by Joe Louis, American hero of the 1940s, and Colin Powell, American hero of the 1990s. *Something* is going on here, a very complex something that I may not succeed in fully teasing out here, although I hope at least to have begun the process of taking its measure.

**Speaking to the NAACP convention in 1922,** a representative of the Negro Press Association urged the organization to do something "to offset the dangerous daily newspaper that ridicules and burlesques us in picture and story." They must recognize that "the rules of yesterday do not apply in this hour of new determination. The old things have passed away, now henceforth and forever. We must be up-to date in thought, word, and deed, or 'lose our ventures.'"[39] These words were spoken at the mere beginning of the consumer society that today colonizes practically the whole of our lives; now image and imagery have achieved a centrality in modern life, enhanced by technological instruments that break down space and time and veritably recreate the public sphere. What are the implications for racial discourse and practice of those transformations?

# 3

# Race, Nation,
# and the Global Economy

I have suggested that my goal is to trace a history not just of racist constraints but also of the conditions of possibility for resistance to racism. The racial regime of the pre-Fordist era was organized to transport racialized groups to places of labor and to keep them physically in place—whether on slave plantations, in sharecroppers' cabins, in convict labor gangs, or tied to indentured contracts. Resistance, individual and collective, most often took the form of escape from those places. Openings within those spaces for frontal attacks on the system of racial oppression occurred only for brief moments, and then usually in the context of life-and-death struggles among the white ruling classes, the American Civil War and Reconstruction being the most obvious such moment.

The racial regime that evolved in the Fordist era was of a very different sort, involving more-complex constraints but also more diverse possibilities for resistance. A high-powered consumer society could be vulnerable to more diversified and effective attack by a demographic minority. First, a mass-production economy called forth mass-production unions whose vulnerability to unskilled scab labor made them more receptive to black members than the traditional crafts-based unions. Second, the state became a powerful and interested player with business and labor in the management of the national economy, making it a potentially decisive arbitrator of private-sector conflicts in which state or political interests were perceived to be at stake. Third, mass-consumption outlets and products depended on national markets, making them vulnerable to locally focused but nationally publicized protest campaigns.

Of these potential vehicles for social change, however, only the targeting of the consumption regime would prove a consistent and effective strategy of social change for African Americans. In some ways the 1915 campaign against *The Birth of a Nation,* flawed though it may have been, was arguably a prototype of the nationwide product-boycott campaigns that would become crucial weapons in later struggles. In any event, consumer boycotts, locally organized but nationally conscious, emerged very early as weapons for racial justice.[1]

By contrast, the other two vehicles of social change not only were more indirect but also proved more ambivalent and uncertain. The federal state would belatedly and almost always ambivalently assume an active role in promoting social change; indeed, sometimes different parts of the state bureaucracy took contrary positions on fostering changes in the status quo.[2] Racial integration of the union movement did not begin until the late 1930s, and the unions' slow and ambivalent embrace of campaigns for racial justice was ultimately stillborn by the early 1950s.[3] Moreover, the most promising and widespread mass movement for racial justice peaked on the eve of fundamental changes in the political-economic base of labor militancy, that is, post-Fordism, which further limited the effectiveness of labor activism as an avenue to social justice. Here I want to probe the constraints that this latest political-economic transformation imposes on our thought as well as our actions, and the necessity to think differently about racial justice in this new era.

## THE MIXED LEGACY OF THE
## CIVIL RIGHTS MOVEMENT

Revisiting the Civil Rights Movement a generation later perhaps enables us to see the ways in which it grew out of, or at least found its material for fashioning, an effective resistance in the changes wrought by the Fordist era. Charles Payne and others have detailed many of the social transformations set in motion by the Second World War, tracing them to the grassroots level of specific families and communities.[4] Others have pushed back to the 1930s and to various movements and personalities, like Ella Baker, who later challenged the dominant black male leadership and organizational structures, in the process laying the basis for the emergence of a youth movement of a special character. Baker's biography also reflects, however, the signal impact of the urban spaces and ideological ferment that shaped her own formative years as she literally trained on Harlem streets for the civil rights revolution to come.[5]

What has emerged from all this is a theory of social-change process consistent with the developments I have outlined earlier. The political movement depended in the first instance on the demographic movement to cities, southern as well as northern. The civil rights revolution was born in northern cities and southern towns, not on plantations, which had imprisoned black folk for much of their history in America, first as slaves and then as share-croppers or leased convicts.

Beyond the grassroots level, we can make similar arguments about the configuration of the organizational leadership. I have emphasized the emergent role of the state, which was crucial in many ways—often despite its own intentions—in reframing the context for social action of all sorts. But we might also note the growing importance in this period of entities we now call NGOs (nongovernmental organizations). Edward Filene had pioneered one such institution, the Twentieth Century Fund, to press his case for state support of a consuming public. But many others flourished, and some of them lent crucial financial support during the 1930s and later to civil rights insurgencies, support that state bureaucracies were unwilling or politically unable to provide. Perhaps the best known of these connections was the Carnegie Corporation's funding of Gunnar Myrdal's 1944 report, *An American Dilemma*, which in its very title altered the intellectual polarity of race relations issues from the older "Negro Problem" to a white problem.[6] For two decades after Myrdal's report the race problem would be discussed as a moral failing of white Americans rather than as a problem of black deficiency. In the 1930s the Garland Fund gave financial support to the NAACP's initial school desegregation efforts; in the 1960s the Taconic and Stern Family funds aided voter registration work in the deep South.[7] The relations between philanthropists and activists were not uncomplicated of course, but they were crucial nonetheless in creating "space" for new strategies and tactics of opposition as well as for mobilization.

Finally, within the South itself mushrooming college enrollments—aided at least in part by the post–Second World War G.I. bill (another form of inadvertent state intervention)—produced a generation prepared to challenge the racial status quo, with their bodies as well as their minds. Again, in this case, too, there was plenty of ambivalence, misdirection, and contradiction. The financially dependent, often pusillanimous administrators of most southern colleges were not only not prepared to support any revolution, but they did all they could to stymie it—threatening, punishing, and expelling student leaders. The tide of change was much too strong for them to resist, however; college students still joined direct action protests in droves and were essential to their success.

In the northern cities there were parallel changes as blacks slowly made their way into industrial workplaces. Here, too, a new space opened up for resisting the racial regime, especially in those industries in which black workers were able to ally themselves with leftist unions. The racism within the American labor movement has been well documented, as has its ambivalent, often hostile relations to the black insurgence of the 1950s and 1960s.[8] Nonetheless, in

the social-geographic landscape of American race relations, unions provided one of the few spaces in which ordinary, working class blacks and whites met, not only to negotiate the racial terrain but to envision a common future.[9]
The closing of those spaces during the reactionary 1980s,
when the union movement declined dramatically, drove
home the implications of their absence, flawed or not.

By and large, however, these developments in the
workplace did not link up with those in the broader community. As we all know, the American Civil Rights Movement unfolded not on shop floors but within a social and
cultural terrain. Not only did its confrontations emerge at
sites of consumption rather than of production, its relation
to the labor movement was by turns weak, ambivalent, and
hostile.[10] There were many reasons for this lack of con-
vergence: the basic conservatism of American labor, the
antileftist purges during the McCarthy era, and the crucial
decisions taken to foster a higher standard of living rather
than to push for more-fundamental social change.[11] For
their part, postwar black leaders inherited a well-earned
distrust of American labor and, with some notable exceptions, had little personal experience in that arena.[12]

The implications of this missed connection are made
evident when we compare the American movements with
their counterparts in Brazil and South Africa a decade or
two later. Sociologist Gay Seidman has shown that at critical moments both in the Brazilian resistance to dictator-
ship in the 1970s and in South African resistance to apart-

heid in the 1980s, decisions were taken to link social and labor movements that had hitherto developed along different trajectories. There are striking similarities in the social and institutional bases of support for the social movements in all three countries: the dramatic urbanization of the population, the power and vulnerabilities of a multinationally-based auto industry, and the existence of nongovernmental entities that trained workers for the insurgence (one in South Africa was very similar to Tennessee's Highlander Folk School). Despite those similarities both the South African and Brazilian movements diverged from the pattern found in the United States. They succeeded in creating broad-based alliances focused not only on material gains but a new relation to the polity, a new citizenship.[13]

That this did not happen in the American movement —at least not on a national level—may well be a determining factor in our current situation. Only in isolated localities did such labor-community alliances unfold, most notably in Memphis in 1967–68, and significantly enough at a time when most observers assumed the Civil Rights Movement was dead.[14] Thus although the U.S. movement put an end to petty apartheid and unleashed the great potential of grassroots communities (some of which was realized or reflected in local and national political campaigns in the ensuing decades), in general its most radical potential was contained. Unable to challenge the political-economic status quo either substantively or conceptually, progressive forces could only fight rearguard actions to defend comparatively limited socioeconomic reforms. At the beginning of the twenty-first century, the social advances won by the 1960s movements are threatened by a broad front of conservative politicians and intellectuals.

Efforts to account for the stalling of progressive change have blamed the socially and financially costly Vietnam War, the backlash of disaffected white working and middle classes, and the shift of focus to the more intractable social problems of northern inner cities. It may be, however, that a broader set of changes framed all these developments, changes that move the discussion beyond the idiosyncrasies of American political realignments.[15] The downturn in progressive politics coincided with the advent of post-Fordist political-economic developments. That the United States was on the leading edge of these developments may help explain why the kinds of alliances possible in Brazil and South Africa never took place in this country. Although the argument would need a great deal more development than it is possible to give it here, we could posit that the kind of labor-social movement alliance that developed in Brazil and South Africa was dependent on conditions produced in a Fordist political economy. Once those conditions ceased to exist, such an alliance faced an immensely more difficult task. By this logic, the best time for an American movement like that in South Africa would have been the 1940s and early 1950s, not the 1960s and 1970s.

## The Post-Fordist Regime

What changed in the late twentieth century that could so profoundly affect movements for social justice and even the very meaning of race?

Obviously, some features of the Fordist era are still quite visible. We still have an economy dominated by multinationals and mass consumption—only even more so. Indeed, our collective economic fate depends on the ever-increasing purchases of automobiles, houses and their furnishings (those closely tracked durable goods). The black role in production via consumption is even more pronounced: Aunt Jemima—a caricature born on the eve of the Fordist era at the 1893 Chicago World's Fair, one in whose bosom the new commerce and the old racial culture were united—has been joined by a plethora of black images and symbols that sell us everything from cars, appliances, and sneakers to getaway vacations. So what's new?

First, since the 1970s, mechanisms for mobilizing capital and productive resources have become more geographically dispersed and yet more institutionally powerful than ever before. Second, the changed geography of economic relations has created new geographies of social and cultural relations as well, quite literally created new spaces of social interaction and imparted new meanings to those relations.[16] As I noted earlier, the creation of global relations of labor and consumption is to some extent constitutive of the advent of modernity, and, as Du Bois suggested, the Atlantic slave trade formed its nexus. In some ways, the changes set in motion in the late twentieth century can be thought of as the further unfolding of that trend; the old is not entirely effaced, the new never entirely new. And yet, there are also radical changes in the time-space dimension of the contemporary world that taken altogether constitute an epistemic shift of historic proportions.

One of the formative moments for the post-Fordist economy was the late 1960s, when major industries seeking lower labor costs and less state regulation moved parts of their production to offshore sites in developing countries, especially to the Caribbean basin and southeast Asia. Within the developed economies this shift in the locus of part of their production paralleled a significant reduction in industrial labor, generally referred to as "deindustrialization." A short time later the partial breakdown of the Bretton Woods international financial system (with respect to currency exchanges) and a Third World debt crisis set in motion radical changes in how investment capital flows were managed and by whom. New financial service providers emerged and, with them, new technologies and technical expertise that fostered innovations in the mobilization and management of capital.[17]

Central to this new economic nexus was a new sociospatial phenomenon that Saskia Sassen has dubbed "global cities." Preeminent among these were cities like

New York, Tokyo, and London that emerged as the service centers for the global economy and enabled a concentration of professional expertise to manage transnational production sites and investment capital flows. These "strategic nodes in the organization of the world economy," as Sassen describes them, brought together new forms of telecommunications and a concentration of complementary professional services (law, accounting, computer programming, and so on) and, with these, created a new internationally linked elite.[18]

Highly paid and highly urbanized, this new elite class of "service workers" required services of its own, leading to the growth of a poor, nonunionized, and largely immigrant working class in those same global cities. Some of these workers are employed in small, sweatshop enterprises making luxury goods for the newly emergent elites. Others are found in the informal economy of household help, gypsy cabdrivers, street vendors, and the like.[19] The immigrants among this group were set in motion toward these global cities by the dislocations prompted by the 1960s and 1970s investments in offshore production in their countries of origin. Much like the industrialization of the early nineteenth century, this one drew women out of traditional economies, first into the wage-labor pools of their native land and then channeled them into immigrant streams and the low and casual wage labor sectors of developed countries. Thus the new service sector and sweatshops in the global cities are strikingly feminized.

Like all immigrant groups historically, these newly displaced workers are prone to self-exploitation, often accepting lower wages and worse working conditions than natives or exploiting unpaid family labor in small shops and stores. All of which sets the stage for new racial tensions between the native-born and immigrant workers in those same global cities.[20]

The scale and nature of this new immigration have recast the problem of race in the modern world.[21] Practically every member of the industrialized economic elite of nations—the so-called G-7 countries—has witnessed politically dangerous and sometimes violent xenophobic outbursts against this new class of immigrants. In much of the developed world the boundaries of race and the boundaries of the nation are politically and conceptually intertwined. Racial issues are also issues of national integrity. Unlike in the early twentieth century, however, race no longer follows a color line. The racialized other may well be white and hail from the Caucasus. Nevertheless, as ostensibly indigenous citizens of the G-7 nations watch their birthrates decline, the need for immigrant labor grows and, with it, a collective anxiety about national *and racial* integrity.[22]

Flowing from these material and socioeconomic changes is a palpable change of our contemporary *habitus*. Some years ago David Harvey suggested that there had been "a sea-change in cultural as well as in political-economic practices." He argued that we now literally experience time and space in new ways and that this experience is related to or expressed in a "time-space compression" in the very organization of contemporary capitalism as well as in our cultural forms and practices.[23] Perhaps Harvey's insights can provide a point of departure for our analysis of the implication this new economic nexus held for racial issues.

I suggested at the outset that there is a new indeterminacy in our measures of racial phenomena and an inscrutability that confounds our understandings of them—all of which is strikingly congruent with descriptions of the deindustrialized, globalized, service economy in which we now live. As Harvey suggests, it is an economy that gives new meaning to the Shakespearean (and later Marxian) line: "All that is solid melts into air." Not only is capital in some sense "fictive," but corporate ownership—and thus responsibility—can itself disappear at "warp speed" into an opaque cyberspace. The stock-market investment instruments called "derivatives," though much maligned recently, reflect the fragmented, recombinant quality of much modern stock ownership. One may own not actual shares of companies, but shares of the rights to buy or sell their stock or their debts at a given moment, under given conditions.[24]

In the novel *Germinal,* Emile Zola satirized the nineteenth-century French stockholders of an oppressive mining company as self-satisfied bourgeois who clipped their coupons but took no responsibility for how the companies they profited from were managed. Today we might well find it practically impossible to trace the actual links between an individual investor and any specific, material corporate enterprise. Meanwhile corporations spend millions to cultivate an image of social responsibility ("goodwill") in general, while making decisions about downsizing and outsourcing that take no responsibility for any actual living communities.

What work does race do in this political economy? First of all, it is clear that although race may indeed do conceptual work in this economy, blacks-as-a-race have no economic role. Despite the dramatic rise in the number of middle-income blacks and, by historical measures, their visible integration into major institutions of the national life, one of the clearest consequences of the transformed economy has been the massive exclusion of blacks from the *formal* economy. And with that exclusion comes the loss of the standard of living and social securities envisaged for industrial workers under a Fordist regime. In contrast to Jesse Jackson's witticism, quoted in the preceding chapter, at the dawn of the twenty-first century, everybody does *not* have a job. Indeed, whereas under earlier regimes racialization was linked to the mobilization of blacks into productive relations, it is now marked by the exclusion of a significant plurality of black people from productive relations.

Of course, this story—of deindustrialization, the service economy, and the so-called underclass—is by now a familiar one. Less familiar, or at least both complicating and suggesting new approaches to this story, are the new relations between production and consumption, between both of these and the state and the nation, and how all of them figure in the delineation of new social spaces and a new transnational racial regime.

As modes of production and consumption undergo radical change, so too do the roles and responsibilities of the state. First, nation-states have become much less autonomous, and in some ways less powerful, in the face of new information technologies and global capital volatility. Eric Hobsbawm has suggested that the palpable growth of nationalism may well reflect the less visible decline of nation-states as structures around which collective identities can be effectively formed.[25] Indeed, governments have surrendered more and more control to multinational bodies like those established by GATT, the World Bank, and the International Monetary Fund in an effort to gain some leverage over market forces. And rather than disciplining the markets, even "first-world" governments are increasingly disciplined *by* the markets. Thus was France rewarded or punished by the financial markets a few years ago according to how far its government succeeded in reducing social welfare spending. And even the all-powerful United States has from time to time found its credit rating and interest rates somewhat dependent on draconian reductions in its welfare state.[26]

The powers that define our livelihoods are increasingly located in transnational processes and follow different social and moral logics. Thus as Zygmunt Bauman puts it:

> The way in which the world economy operates today (and there is today a genuine world economy) favours state organisms that cannot effectively impose conditions under which economy runs; economy is effectively transnational —and in relation to virtually any state, big or small, most of economic assets crucial for the daily life of its population are "foreign." The divorce between political autarchy (real or imaginary) and economic autarky seems to be irrevocable.[27]

At the dawn of the twenty-first century, not only does everybody not have a job, but the conventional economic wisdom is that it would be bad for the economy if everybody did. Some structural unemployment is necessary, we are told—to keep inflation down. Every interest-rate hike approved by the Federal Reserve gives renewed credence to the old Marxian charge that the welfare of capital depends on maintaining "a reserve army of unemployed."[28]

Other parts of the state apparatus, traditionally more sympathetic to the needs of labor and the poor, are under increasing pressure to withdraw their support. The impact of such policies on the poor are obvious, but the recently emergent black middle class is especially at risk as state functions are retrenched. This historically novel class differentiation within the black population—an upper middle class, a working class, and the so-called underclass— was highly dependent on the expansion of state activity and expenditures under the Fordist regime. Thus the employment of that middle class is heavily concentrated in the public and/or public-contracted sector; and its wealth consists largely of salaries rather than financial assets.[29] A great deal of attention has been given recently to the bifurcation of the American black class experience; that is, that there are historically high levels of both social-economic inclusion *and* exclusion.[30] We might complicate that image by noting the very real vulnerability at both ends of the class structure.

The meanings, anomalies, and ambivalences produced by these transnational pressures are complicated further by the fundamental, continuing changes in our *habitus*—our everyday, lived, built, and perceptual environments. Housing, one of the new terrains of racial confrontation that emerged in the Fordist era, is no longer a simple matter of segregated neighborhoods but of gated communities, a phenomenon of privatized urban space that has emerged in locales as disparate as Los Angeles and São Paulo.[31] Unlike the images from the *Sweet* case and Detroit in the 1950s, however, such communities may well have at least a token black or other minority presence. Are they, by virtue of that fact, any less racial?

## RACE AND RACISM IN AN
## ECONOMY OF SYMBOLS

Just as Fordism eventually changed the way people lived and how they thought about how they lived, so has/will

the post-Fordist social order. Musing over whether the
new inequality has produced new social forms, Saskia
Sassen concludes that the new global-city elites have embraced an ideology of consumption strikingly different
from those found in Fordist-era suburbs. "Style, high
prices, and an ultraurban context characterize the new
ideology and practice of consumption, rather than func-
tionality, low prices, and suburban settings."[32] Dip-
lomatic historian Walter LaFeber finds a radically new
mode of cultural transmission among nations. Cultural
influences were once carried across national boundaries
by migrants, elite travelers, or a literate readership. Now
via television satellites culture moves "with the speed of
sound," reaching billions of people in an instant.[33]

In both time and space, local and global venues, the
meanings, modalities, and consequences of consumption
decisions have fundamentally changed. No longer simply
a matter of Henry Ford's workers having the means to buy
an automobile or a house to keep the economy purring,
consumption now permeates—even regulates perhaps—
practically all aspects of social life, including our politics.
"Values" and "identities" have become consumables—
they are packaged, advertised, and purchased. Our existence has never before been so commodified; our understanding, our knowing never before so dependent on representations of, symbols of putatively underlying realities
that are not otherwise apparent; our perceptual universe
never before so fragmented and fluid. Our social world is

littered with the cultural equivalents of financial "derivatives."

Is it possible that the whole complex, post-Fordist system depends upon this *habitus,* much as the fragmenting, reductive qualities of the computer are necessary to construct a stock market derivative? Our fin-de-siècle political economy simultaneously promotes "homogenization" and "differentiation." It requires each of us individually to desire different goods that signify our distinction and individuality; but it also requires us to accept the same basis of evaluation, the same kind of commodity so that production can be viable.[34]

In a global marketplace, therefore, all commodities are cultural, and they thrive on real and simulated differences—on containable signs of difference, on distinction. A pair of bluejeans, Nike running shoes, Suchard chocolates, a BMW are not just clothing, food, or a means of transportation. Among other things they variously connote American casualness, a virile leisure class, the French "smart" set, well-being and power.

All this suggests that in this post-Fordist world we are more dependent than ever on a veritable "economy of symbols."[35] Of course, the unwritten codes embedded in signs and symbols have always been crucial to our ability to negotiate our way through our everyday worlds. But the material and psychic shocks of the time compression of this era have intensified the process of such symbolic negotiation.[36]

Could it be that in such a marketplace, black bodies—
no longer a means of production—have become a means
of consumption? Could it be that Michael Jordan, the
model for Suchard chocolates, Grace Jones modeling *as
an automobile*[37]—or for that matter, Colin Powell—notwithstanding their general attractiveness otherwise can
now become meaningful as signs, not despite their blackness but because of it? Could it be that the issue now is less
the utter ignorance of other cultures, as in times past, but
too great a surface (sound-bite) familiarity; less stereotypes of the other than the voracious consumption of its
metonymic parts? It is difficult, perhaps impossible, to
answer such questions definitively. Difficult to know even
how such propositions might be tested. A closer look at
some of the icons of the new economy might help us tease
out some of the work that race does.

I suggested earlier that it might be possible to trace an
interesting trajectory from Jack Johnson at the opening of
the Fordist era through Joe Louis at its maturation (inci-
dentally Louis also worked in the auto plants of Detroit
before turning to professional boxing) down to Michael
Jordan today. Already evident in those earlier black sports
figures was the tendency to turn them into texts on which
the nation could work out its tensions and anxieties—
much like the work minstrel shows did in the antebellum
era. The articulation of race and consumption was merely
emergent in the Johnson-Louis era, however. In the selling of Michael Jordan it has come full circle.[38]

Not only is the Jordan phenomenon rife with the fragmentation and contradiction discussed earlier, it is thoroughly embedded in and reflective of the post-Fordist economy. Notwithstanding the incredible basketball skills, competitive character, and magnetic personality Jordan brings to the mix, his professional success is ultimately built on two powerful multinational capital enterprises— the National Basketball Association and Nike. (And in recent years they, of course, have been built largely on him.) Through the marriage of new communications technology, aggressive capitalist expansion, and image, both of these enterprises flourished in the late twentieth century. The NBA merged television and slick advertising to transform a sport in crisis in the 1980s into a domestic and international cultural and economic marvel in the 1990s. By the peak of Jordan's career in 1997, the number of TV sets per hundred of the world's people had doubled. Consequently, when Jordan announced his retirement from basketball on January 13, 1999, a Japanese newspaper banner headline read: "Jordan Retires! Shock Felt around the World." Although basketball was a minor sport in Japan, Air Jordan sneakers sold for as much as $1,000 a pair and "were collected like jewels."[39]

Nike, meanwhile, though founded in little Beavertown, Oregon, secured its startup capital, made its shoes, and earned most of its profits overseas. Moving from one Asian country to another in search of lower wages, Nike was a veritable archetype of a post-Fordist multinational.

In a well-worn pattern, noted earlier, its overseas labor force was heavily feminized; 90 percent of the workers in its Vietnamese plant, for example, were women.[40]

But if Michael Jordan's career was made by Nike's multinational reach, Nike's success was just as surely built on Jordan's image. Indeed, that image, in silhouette, is copyrighted by Nike. Some of the troubling aspects of the enterprises built on Jordan's image are well known. The firm paid Jordan $20 million annually to promote its products, which was more than the total annual wages earned by Indonesian workers who made the shoe. Little girls in those same plants earn the equivalent of under $2 for an eleven-hour day, making shoes that sell for $70 to $150 in the West and that cost $5.60 to make. Michael Jordan is merely a cog—albeit a highly paid cog—in the complex machinery of the post-Fordist economy, however. Through that well-known logo based on the image of his black body soaring through the air is revealed the now intimate connection between a new international political economy, a transnational pattern of consumption, and black identity. Jordan, it has been observed, "was an image much like the Swoosh." Or, as Phil Knight, the entrepreneur behind Nike's success, explains it: "You can't explain much in 60 seconds, but when you show Michael Jordan, you don't have to. People already know a lot about him. It's that simple."[41] What Jordan sold was not just a product but a life-style. "Just do it!" is now familiar to youth across the globe and needs no translation.

What can it mean that kids all over the world, in many different languages, can say, "I want to be like Mike"? Does this phenomenon still lie within the orbit of the racial? Just posing the question might be startling to some because Jordan is widely celebrated as a figure who transcends race. With some poignancy his friend and fellow basketball great, Julius Irving, observed that Jordan seemed "less a person than something of a 24-hour commodity."[42] The conjunction of those two observations—a person who transcends race; a commodified personality—may well speak to a central issue in the social transformation that has engaged us. What can it mean that a commodified Jordan "transcends" race when just a few years earlier the premier black professional players were routinely denied endorsement contracts because it was assumed that their endorsements would not sell products to whites?[43] Indeed what does it mean to transcend race in a sport from which blacks were first excluded and then had their eventual success attributed to racial biology?[44]

Certainly, nineteenth- and early-twentieth-century meanings of race and racism are not sufficient to explain such phenomena. One of the standard definitions of racism assumes that it is always a response to an alleged inferiority of the racialized other,[45] but contemporary racial images often refer merely to difference, exoticism, and sometimes even to an ostensible superiority.

And with that observation we can return to that other enigmatic icon of the new racial regime, Colin Powell.

Powell's successful, if brief, courtship of American public opinion has also been attributed to his ability to transcend race—the "un-Negro."[46] But again, what can it mean to claim that Powell transcends race in a political culture that is saturated with racially coded images and language? Just three years before Powell's phantom candidacy unfolded, a political observer began an analysis of American politics with the following characterization: "considerations of race are now deeply embedded in the strategy and tactics of politics, in competing concepts of the function and responsibility of government, and in each voter's conceptual structure of moral and partisan identity."[47]

But leaving aside the poisonous racial climate in which Powell's potential candidacy unfolded, any claims to racial transcendence beg the question: Why Powell? If the answer is character or the appeal of his biography, then both his race and the overcoming of racism are part of the story. Or, alternatively, it is a life story—like Jordan's—ostensibly in which race "didn't matter." Either way, a crucial "truth" about the national character and identity appears to be affirmed—its justice, its fairness, its color-blindness. Though invisible, race does its work. It is conceivable that the need for that work to be done reflects the difficulty in defining and sustaining an integrated, psychologically satisfying identity under contemporary social conditions.[48] As at other moments in American history, then, race is the medium through which other fundamental conflicts in the social system are "lived" and "fought through."

It remains to be seen whether some of this work that race does today, and will no doubt continue to do, is relatively innocuous or harmful. Which way it cuts may depend on whether and how the relatively benign images of the Michael Jordans and Colin Powells of the world articulate with—or perhaps are actually dependent on—those of ghetto youth and "welfare queens."

This issue may well be the key to unraveling the meaning of race in the twenty-first century. In sorting through all this we might again take note of the Geertzian observation that a game is often more than merely a game. Likewise it may be that symbols cannot always be confined to the safe terrain of the merely symbolic. So mundane an aspect of our everyday lives as the clothing we wear, whose labels are sewn onto the *outside* of the garment, suggests the pervasive link between symbol and the hard currency of the economic. When ghetto kids kill each other for a pair of brand-name sneakers, it brings home that this economy of symbols is not just serious; it's deadly serious.[49]

I introduced this discussion with the observation that, like Du Bois, we might need to reach an understanding of our present and future by reexamining our past. Even as I emphasize the novelty of the present moment in history—a new political economy and a new racial regime—I am also cognizant of shards of our racial past sedimented in this brave new world. Take the slogan of the Memphis movement that unfolded in the twilight days of the civil rights era, its possibility for catching and shaping the winds of change nationally perhaps snuffed out with the life of Martin Luther King Jr. on that fateful balcony. In 1968 the Memphis workers marched under the banner "I am a man." The slogan strikingly echoes the one emblazoned on nineteenth-century abolitionist banners protesting the slave trade. For Memphis workers it invoked the issue of identity, indeed a claim—in the broadest terms—to citizenship, to membership in the polity as the covering rationale for what was essentially a labor action. For victims of the slave trade it was a claim to, a plea for, recognition of a common humanity.

In each of these senses it resonates yet again with the condition of the most recent victims of the racialization process in this global economy. I mentioned earlier that sweatshop workers in our era are to be found not just in East Asia but also in East Los Angeles. I was referring to a case brought to light a few years ago of Mexican and Thai women laboring under slavelike conditions in sweatshops in Los Angeles, making goods for the luxury consumer market. The word "slavelike" in this case is not hyperbole. Once discovered, these workers brought suit under laws based on the Thirteenth Amendment to the Constitution—the one outlawing slavery. They are not the last such workers to be discovered in such straits; and all such discoveries continue to raise the issue of how race, labor, and citizenship are to be articulated in the twenty-first century.[50]

**In some sense, perhaps,** these poignant images take us full circle from the economy of symbols to a hard-edged political economy—or more accurately perhaps to where race and political economy join up with the superconsumption of our post-Fordist era. But we have also, in some more disturbing sense, returned to those ships plying their way across the Atlantic laden with human cargo—humans shorn of a place in a bewilderingly transformed world. Perhaps, more than ever, we can feel—and in more than simply a historical sense—our fate linked with theirs.

# Epilogue:
# The Future
# of Race

B y the time my one-year-old daughter has reached her eighteenth birthday, fully a century after her grandfather's birth, the issues discussed in these pages may be of mere historical interest, reflecting a time long since passed when visions of the future were more blurred and imaginations more limited. Perhaps African Americans will no longer be at the center of racial debate and policy, much as the intensity of Americans' interest in Native Americans in the nineteenth century declined in the twentieth. Like Native Americans, too, perhaps blacks will have become less the object of deep social and political concern than of symbolic manipulation; some signs of such a trend are discernible even in today's symbolic economy of racial imagining. Perhaps other racialized groups among a now globalized labor force will have taken their place, perhaps not. Or perhaps race will no longer even be an issue.

Perhaps. But two decades will probably not have completely altered the themes and patterns evident in a tortured history now four centuries old. Indeed, as in the past, the enduring power of race may lie in its ambiguity, its mutability, its parasitism, all of which continue to make effective resistance to it difficult. If we assume that racism may still limit African Americans' aspirations and life chances in the year 2017, what can we say to our children today to arm them for the inevitable struggles of that future?

We might begin by telling them that for all its camouflage, racism can nonetheless be recognized by the work it does, by its effects. Any ideology, any ostensible truth, any revered common sense that stifles their chances for self-realization because of who they are is likely to be racism, sexism, or both.

We can tell them that however formidable and enduring the noxious weed of racism may seem, the ground that nourishes it can also destroy it. This is the paradox embedded in the preceding pages: racial ideologies and constraints are shaped by the historical-material moment—the *habitus*—of a given era, but that same *habitus* provides materials and means for resistance to those ideologies and constraints. In the era of bound labor, slaves found ways to break their chains and escape. In the Fordist era, consumers interrupted the free flow of goods and services on which the economy depended. Perhaps in a post-Fordist era so imbued with racial imagery and so dependent on global networks of communication and labor recruitment, we can also forge global networks of resistance. In a political economy so dependent on the manipulation of symbols and imagery, perhaps we can simply refuse to be manipulated and create alternative images of a nonracialized future.

But such a response exposes a second paradox: only those acting outside the dominant racial ideas and constraints of their era can effectively seize the means of resistance to them. The tiny minority who act outside the constraints of their times in fact help to define those times. We must be able to imagine a different future if we are to be able to change the present and thus shape that future.

We cannot abolish racism while trapped within its own conceptual terrain.

From a distance statements like this may seem to blur into those of many contemporary neoconservatives who argue for a color-blind approach to racial problems. They are a mixed lot: some seem to think that American society is already color-blind, while others think that it can soon become so; some make patently racist arguments, while others seem to be genuinely struggling to find a way out, though apparently embarrassed by what a messy job it is to clean up racism's mess. Nonetheless, most of them seem skeptical of the necessity for or desirability of righting racial wrongs through state action (the main way collective will is expressed in modern democratic societies). In my view such positions fly in the face of the overwhelming contemporary evidence that racism permeates every institution, every pore of everyday life. Justice in our courts, earnings on our jobs, whether we have a job at all, the quality of our life, the means and timing of our death—all form the stacked deck every child born black must take up to play the game of life. To later generations these wrongs—and the need for collective efforts to right them—will be as clear as the wrongs of slavery were to those born after 1865, or of segregation to those born after 1964.

When I say that we must move from racism's terrain in order to break its spell, therefore, I mean something very different. Martin Luther King Jr. was fond of saying that "the moral arc of the universe is long but it bends toward justice." Trouble is, the life of any given individual is considerably shorter than that of the universe. Our children don't have time to wait for the cosmic flywheel of justice to right itself or, for that matter, for the government to do its job. Therefore, notwithstanding the tenacious grip, the heavy weight of racism on every institution, on every discourse, on every relationship, black children *must* live *as if* the world were otherwise, as if it were color-blind. They must claim their rightful lives now, living as if race were not a constraint on life, as if they were not "black."

By that I do not mean that African-American children should deny their blackness—nothing would be gained and much lost by such a response to racism. Rather I mean that they must deny the meanings now attributed to being black. Or, to frame yet another paradox, they must claim their "blackness" yet live beyond it. They must not confound race with peoplehood. Taking pride in our ancestors' histories and struggles is the beginning of our self-fashioning—it makes us who we are. But a legacy should be a point of departure, not a destination. There is a difference between being nourished by our history and being consumed by it.

Certainly the history of African Americans contains some complex and difficult truths. Historically, to be African American has been to live on the razor's edge of ambiguity and seeming indeterminacy. The homespun proverbs abound: "to make bricks without straw," "to make a way out of no way." Only our singers, our poets, and a few of our intellectuals have had the wit to name it. Du Bois called it a "double consciousness"; Ralph Ellison hailed "the harsh discipline" of African-American cultural life. More often an unnamed yet lived experience, it is a timeless resource embedded in our personal histories and memories. From that lived experience come, to borrow Toni Morrison's haunting phrase, "stories to grow on." Stories for our children to seize and claim as their own. Stories of a people who pulled something from deep within themselves that little in their visible history and circumstance would have seemed to warrant.

**What, then, can I tell my daughter** if the problem of the twenty-first century is still the color-line? "Like many who have gone before you, you must struggle against injustice with all your might. You must refuse to be racialized or to racialize others. But at the same time you must also live as if the world were otherwise. You must reach out and claim it as your own. I know that is a lot to ask. It will certainly require a difficult heroism and a subtle resistance, as well as exposure to the risk of being misunderstood by your peers and elders. But perhaps . . . just perhaps . . . when enough people do as you do, racism will indeed have no future."

# Notes

INTRODUCTION

1. W. E. B. Du Bois, *Souls of Black Folk* (Chicago: McClurg, 1903), 13. An earlier version of this thought ("the color line belts the world" and "the social problem of the twentieth century is to be the relation of the civilized world to the dark races of mankind") was articulated in Du Bois's "The Present Outlook for the Dark Races of Mankind," AME *Church Review* 17 (October 1900): 95–100.

2. What I have described here are the dominant popular ideas and most common academic referents for racism, notwithstanding that scholars meanwhile have been exploring more complex forms of and meanings embedded within racial phenomena, including interracial interactions and the positive deployment of racial stereotypes. Indeed, some insights from these works have been useful in this exploration of our own time. See, for example, Eric Lott, *Love and Theft: Blackface Minstrelsy and the American Working Class* (New York: Oxford University Press, 1993); Martha Hodes, *White Women, Black Men: Illicit Sex in the Nineteenth-Century South* (New Haven: Yale University Press, 1997); Leora Auslander and Thomas C. Holt, "Sambo à Paris: Race et racisme dans l'iconographie du quotidien" (Manuscript).

3. For a contemporaneous assessment that was more optimistic about Powell's chances, see Steven Stark, "President Powell?" *Atlantic Monthly* 272, no. 4 (October 1993): 22–29.

4. Can the striking difference in the receptions of Powell's candidacy and Jackson's be explained simply by the difference in timing, in their respective politics, or in their careers? Although all these factors may be pertinent, my discussion of the role of race in contemporary life will suggest a more complex situation. For a subtle sketch of Powell, his moment, and the contrast with Jackson, see Henry Louis Gates Jr., *Thirteen Ways of Looking at a Black Man* (New York: Vintage Books, 1997), 72–102.

5. "Second Ex-Paratrooper Gets Life in North Carolina Racial Kill-ings," *New York Times,* 13 May 1997, A17.

6. The fictional part of this conjuncture is based on two actual incidents that occurred a decade apart, in New York City in the spring of 1987 (when Michael Jackson was at the height of his popularity) and in Chicago in March 1997.

7. The first category of commentary has expanded dramatically in recent years as the political right seeks to roll back and destroy affirmative action. The connection between a narrow definition of racism and programmatic retrenchment is made most explicit by Dinesh D'Souza, who argues that there is a legitimate distinction between a presumably unacceptable irrational racism based on biology and an acceptable "rational" discrimination based on the cultural deficiencies of blacks. By his lights the latter should not be the object of state action. *The End of Racism: Principles for a Multiracial Society* (New York: Free Press, 1995), 28, 286–287, 537–546. A prominent example of the second category is Robert Miles, *Racism* (London: Routledge, 1989), 41–68. Miles worries over processes by which the concept of racism has been inflated so that there is no way to distinguish it from all other ideas and acts that make biological or pseudobiological claims, as with nationalism or sexism. But it seems possible, nonetheless, to rhetorically label a broad range of actions that share a common feature (like biological determinism) as racist and then focus on certain historically distinct varieties of that phenomenon. The problem of definition also inflects many discussions that attempt to draw clear distinctions between racial effects and class effects, a distinction this book will, at least indirectly, call into question.

8. Some of the most cogent and persuasive expressions of this view are found in seminal articles by Stuart Hall, Barbara Fields, and Evelyn Brooks Higginbotham: Stuart Hall, "Race, Articulation and Societies Structured in Dominance," in *Sociological Theories: Race and Colonialism* (Paris: UNESCO, 1980), 305–345; Barbara Jeanne Fields, "Slavery, Race, and Ideology in the United States of America," *New Left Review* 181 (May–June 1990): 95–118; Evelyn Brooks Higginbotham, "African-American Women's History and the Metalanguage of Race," *Signs* 17 (Winter 1992).

9. For a fascinating examination of how the Commonwealth of

Virginia's Board of Vital Statistics was aggressively deployed to maintain racial purity during the early twentieth century, see Steve Porter, "Drawing and Policing the Color Line: Racial Classification in Creating and Maintaining Power at the Virginia Bureau of Vital Statistics, 1924–1946" (M.A. thesis, University of Chicago, 1998).

10. For one example of such slippage, see Winthrop D. Jordan, *White over Black: Historical Origins of Racism in the United States* (New York: Oxford University Press, 1968), 257. Also see my earlier commentary on this problem in "Explaining Race in American History," in *Imagined Histories: American Historians Interpret the Past,* ed. Anthony Molho and Gordon S. Wood (Princeton: Princeton University Press, 1998), 107–119.

11. For a provocative discussion of this phenomenon see Kwame Anthony Appiah, "The Uncompleted Argument: Du Bois and the Illusion of Race," *Critical Inquiry* 12 (Autumn 1985): 21–37.

12. Etienne Balibar, "Is There a 'Neo-Racism'?" in *Race, Nation, Class: Ambiguous Identities,* ed. Etienne Balibar and Immanuel Wallerstein (London: Verso, 1991), 21.

13. Two recent volumes addressing this crisis have been especially illuminating: Sherry B. Ortner, ed., *The Fate of "Culture": Geertz and Beyond* (Berkeley: University of California Press, 1999); and Victoria E. Bonnell and Lynn Hunt, eds., *Beyond the Cultural Turn: New Directions in the Study of Society and Culture* (Berkeley: University of California Press, 1999). Much of this discussion begins, of course, with the seminal work of Clifford Geertz, whose entire career has been devoted to exploring and delineating just what "the cultural" is. See *The Interpretation of Cultures: Selected Essays* (New York: Basic Books, 1973).

14. Very helpful to me in working through the problem in these pages is an article by William H. Sewell Jr., "The Concept(s) of Culture," in Bonnell and Hunt, *Beyond the Cultural Turn,* 35–61.

15. John Rex, *Race and Ethnicity* (Buckingham, U.K.: Open University, 1986), 16–17, 36, 80.

16. The term "ethnicity" appears to have been coined by W. Lloyd Warner and Paul S. Lunt in their 1942 book, *Yankee City,* in which they argued that ethnicity could have a biological as well as a cultural component. The blacks in Yankee City represented the biological end of the spectrum of ethnicity and the Irish the cultural

end, notwithstanding their concession that the Irish and the blacks shared the same culture. "The Yankee City Negro's culture comes from a Yankee tradition, but the group's biological differences provide a symbol around which social differences are defined and evaluated. The Irish maintain certain social usages that differentiate them in varying degrees from the whole community. The other groups fall in between these two extremes." Biology here is symbolic, but it also has a certain fixed quality over which the people so designated have little control. Culture on the other hand is manipulable; the Irish "maintain" certain "social usages" that mark their difference from others in the community. Presumably when they *choose* to stop differentiating themselves—give up their lodges or payments to the IRA—they will simply fall back into the mainstream of Yankee City culture. W. Lloyd Warner and Paul S. Lunt, "Ethnicity," in *Theories of Ethnicity: A Classical Reader,* ed. Werner Sollors (New York: University Press, 1996), 13–16.

17. Werner Sollors, "Ethnicity," in *Critical Terms for Literary Study,* ed. Frank Lentricchia and Thomas McLaughlin (Chicago: University of Chicago Press, 1990), 288. See also Sollors, *Theories of Ethnicity,* x–xliv; and William Petersen, "Concepts of Ethnicity," in *The Harvard Encyclopedia of American Ethnic Groups,* ed. Stephan Thernstrom (Cambridge, Mass.: Harvard University Press, 1986), 234–242.

18. Werner Sollors, ed., *The Invention of Ethnicity* (New York: Oxford University Press, 1989); Kathleen Neils Conzen, "Ethnicity as Festival Culture: Nineteenth-Century German America on Parade," in ibid., 44–76.

19. James Baldwin, "On Being 'White' . . . and Other Lies," *Essence,* April 1984. One of the first of the recent investigations of the phenomenon Baldwin described is David R. Roediger, *The Wages of Whiteness: Race and the Making of the American Working Class* (London: Verso, 1991).

20. A useful discussion on this point, which also takes the discussion outside the American and European context, is John Comaroff's "Of Totemism and Ethnicity: Consciousness, Practice and the Signs of Inequality," *Ethnos* 52, no. 3–4 (1987): 301–323.

21. The subject of discussion was my paper at a 1995 conference on historiography in San Marino. The paper was later published as "Explaining Race in American History."

22. The exception is a special issue on the historicization of race and racism in *Historia Social* (Valencia, Spain) 2 (Fall 1995).

23. See Foucault's idea of historical analysis as archaeology in *The Archaeology of Knowledge,* trans. A. M. Sheridan Smith (New York: Pantheon, 1972).

24. Hall, "Race, Articulation and Societies," 308.

25. Throughout this book I use "articulate" to convey a sense of a relationship or linkage between two or more systems (or structured sets of relations) that are at least partly self-contained and autonomous but that act upon or condition each other. The term, left largely undefined in its original usage by Louis Althusser, has been subsequently deployed in multiple senses, though usually in reference to the "articulation" between modes of production. In some hands the concept conveys determinism, but its etymological roots ("to relate to" and "to speak for") suggest an interconnectedness of domains that is also historically contingent. A useful discussion of both the history and possibilities of the term is found in Hall, "Race, Articulation and Societies," 319–321, 324–332.

26. Ibid., 337.

27. I have traced these developments in Du Bois's thought in "The Political Uses of Alienation: W. E. B. Du Bois on Politics, Race, and Culture, 1903–1940," *American Quarterly* 42 (June 1990): 301–323.

28. My use of the term *habitus* draws upon but deviates somewhat from that of Bourdieu in *Outline of a Theory of Practice,* trans. Richard Nice (Cambridge: Cambridge University Press, 1977). What I take from Bourdieu is the idea of social action in which the material and the symbolic or representational are interactive and mutually supportive without one's being reduced to the other. But most important is the understanding that there are behaviors and practices that are not controlled by conscious intention but that are conventional—i.e., taken-for-granted rules and rationales—just as a traffic light is taken for granted; and, finally, that these conventions are programmatic without being deterministic; that is, innovation, contingency, creativity can change—subtly or overtly—the rules of the game: people occasionally run red lights. See also Randal Johnson's introduction to Bourdieu's *The Field of Cultural Production* (New York: Columbia University Press, 1993).

29. The temporal framework here is indebted to David Harvey, *The*

*Condition of Postmodernity: An Enquiry into the Origins of Cultural Change* (Oxford: Oxford University Press, 1989). Of course, the idea of a Fordist economy is much older, being the subject of discussion by, among others, Antonio Gramsci in *The Prison Notebooks*.

30. Meeting in Bretton Woods, New Hampshire, in July 1944, the Bretton Woods Conference (officially known as the United Nations Monetary and Financial Conference) drew representatives from forty-four countries to devise a postwar global financial system, with the goal of stabilizing currency exchanges and thereby enlarging world trade. The International Monetary Fund (IMF) and World Bank were established as a result of this conference.

# 1. Racial Identity and the Project of Modernity

1. Stuart Hall, "Race, Articulation and Societies Structured in Dominance," in *Sociological Theories: Race and Colonialism* (Paris: UNESCO, 1980), 305–345.

2. David Theo Goldberg, *Racist Culture: Philosophy and the Politics of Meaning* (Oxford: Blackwell, 1993).

3. As Goldberg puts it: "Race is one of the central conceptual inventions of modernity"; ibid., 3. For a concrete and intriguing examination of how a very modern institution can reproduce racist ideologies, see Nayan Shah, *Lives at Risk: Epidemics and Race in San Francisco's Chinatown* (Berkeley: University of California Press, forthcoming).

4. For a useful summary of the timing issue, including a discussion of the gendered aspects of such conceptions and definitions, see Rita Felski, *The Gender of Modernity* (Cambridge, Mass.: Harvard University Press, 1995), 12–15.

5. Focusing on intellectual history, Michael T. Ryan argues that Europeans were surprisingly uncurious about the new worlds they encountered, and simply fitted them within existing mental frameworks. See "Assimilating New Worlds in the Sixteenth and Seventeenth Centuries," *Comparative Studies of Society and History* 23 (1981): 519–538. Perhaps the link between European encounters with the Other and sixteenth-century concerns—both popular and

"scientific"—with wonders and monsters might be one fruitful way to probe this mentalité. For brief but suggestive references to such connections, see Ivan Hannaford, *Race: The History of an Idea in the West* (Baltimore: Johns Hopkins University Press, 1996). For the content and timing of the "wonders" phenomenon generally, see Katherine Park and Lorraine J. Daston, "Unnatural Conceptions: The Study of Monsters in Sixteenth- and Seventeenth-Century France and England," *Past and Present* 92 (August 1981): 20–54.

6. Many of Du Bois's insights on this general phenomenon are found in *Black Reconstruction* (1935) and *Dusk of Dawn* (1940). For Eric Williams', see *Capitalism and Slavery* (1944; reprint, New York: Capricorn, 1966); for C. L. R. James's, *The Black Jacobins: Toussaint L'Ouverture and the San Domingo Revolution* (1938; reprint, New York: Viking Press, 1963).

7. See Laurent Dubois, "A Colony of Citizens: Revolution and Slave Emancipation in the French Caribbean, 1789–1802" (Ph.D. diss., University of Michigan, 1998); and Julius S. Scott III, " 'The Common Wind': Currents of Afro-American Communication in the Era of the Haitian Revolution" (Ph.D. diss., Duke University, 1986).

8. Frederick Cooper, Thomas C. Holt, and Rebecca J. Scott, *Beyond Slavery: Explorations of Race, Labor, and Citizenship in Postemancipation Societies* (Chapel Hill: University of North Carolina Press, 2000), 1–32.

9. A striking exposition of the linkages between New World production and Old World consumption can be found in Sidney W. Mintz, *Sweetness and Power: The Place of Sugar in Modern History* (New York: Viking, 1985).

10. An exemplary study of these kinds of mutual influences and interactions is Frederick Cooper's *Decolonization and African Society: The Labor Question in French and British Africa* (Cambridge: Cambridge University Press, 1996).

11. The example of Jews in medieval Europe is an obvious one here, but also one that helps draw some important distinctions between the modern and earlier eras. See the later discussion of Jewish expulsions from Spain, and also Hannaford, *Race*, 87–126.

12. Cooper, Holt, and Scott, *Beyond Slavery*, 1–32, 151–156.

13. For discussion of the idea of modernity as an ongoing "project," see Maurizio Passerin d'Entrèves and Seyla Benhabib, eds., *Habermas*

14. *and the Unfinished Project of Modernity: Critical Essays on* The Philosophical Discourse of Modernity (Cambridge: Polity Press, 1996).

14. The connection between secularization and racial thought in early modern England is suggested by Winthrop D. Jordan, *White over Black: Historical Origins of Racism in the United States* (New York: Oxford University Press, 1968), 216–265.

15. Although it is unclear just what aspects of modern thought he underscores as most relevant, Goldberg is certainly correct when he asserts that modernity's radical intellectual project had to precede and give form to racism; *Racist Culture,* 53, 62, 146–147.

16. Ibid., 81.

17. David Brion Davis' work makes this point very powerfully. See especially *The Problem of Slavery in the Age of Revolution, 1770–1823* (Ithaca: Cornell University Press, 1975).

18. Goldberg, *Racist Culture,* 81. This is also a theme to which a number of students of ethnicity allude. See Werner Sollors, ed., *Theories of Ethnicity: A Classical Reader* (New York: New York University Press, 1996), xvi–xxi.

19. For examples see George Johnson, "Ethical Fears Aside, Science Plunges On," *New York Times,* 7 December 1997; and Andrew Pollack, "We Can Engineer Nature. But Should We?" *New York Times,* 6 February 2000.

20. Among many such texts, see Zygmunt Bauman, *Modernity and the Holocaust* (Ithaca: Cornell University Press, 1989).

21. Although I find Foucault's paradigm provocative and useful, I also have criticisms of it, which can be found in my intervention at the conference introducing its first French edition, "Comment on Foucault's War of the Races," in *Lectures de M. Foucault,* vol. 1: *De la guerre des races au racisme d'état. A propos de "il faut defendre la société,"* ed. Jean-Claude Zancarini (Lyons: ENS Editions, 2000). For a more extended description and a perceptive analysis of the lectures, see Ann Laura Stoler, *Race and the Education of Desire: Foucault's History of Sexuality and the Colonial Order of Things* (Durham, N.C.: Duke University Press, 1995).

22. Most of Foucault's lectures are devoted to tracing the language of racial struggle from the medieval to the modern era, of which I can give but a very brief synopsis here. In the premodern era, he argues,

various insurgents struggling against the authoritarian claims of monarchical sovereigns fashioned an oppositional narrative of origin in which they pitted "the people" against an illegitimate "Other." In the process they constituted a binary discursive field on which two races were arrayed against each other. (But "races" here should be read as nations, and in some cases as classes.) As we move into the modern era the state emerges as the site (at once centralized and dispersed) where the nation is constituted through distinct but interrelated processes of discipline (making one do what power desires) and normalization (defining what is in fact desirable). The boundaries at issue are no longer historical ancestry but biological fitness. Race is no longer binary but singular.

23. There are persuasive arguments—found as early as the 1930s in the writings of C. L. R. James (*Black Jacobins*) and W. E. B. Du Bois (*Black Reconstruction*)—that America, the Americas, and the American slave plantations were sites of some of the earliest modern experiments in repression, that they produced the first truly modern workers, and that the first instances of modern angst about identity and difference appear among their inhabitants.

24. I am not, of course, suggesting that Foucault's modern state be subsumed under the slave plantation or vice versa, or that they are entirely comparable. I am merely suggesting that some crucial features of the former may have been anticipated by the latter: first, the method or mode of biological and economic calculation toward totalitarian socioeconomic ends and, second, the "will to power" that can render to such calculations the moral status of a social good. The literature is vast here, but two very different works that emphasize the planters' "calculation" are Howard Temperly, "Capitalism, Slavery, and Ideology," *Past and Present* 75 (May 1977): 94–118; and Robert W. Fogel and Stanley L. Engerman, *Time on the Cross: The Economics of American Negro Slavery* (Boston: Little, Brown, 1974). See also Richard Dunn, *Sugar and Slaves: The Rise of the Planter Class in the English West Indies, 1624–1713* (Chapel Hill: University of North Carolina Press, 1972). Such features of modern rationality are powerfully and artfully rendered with the character Schoolteacher in Toni Morrison's novel *Beloved*.

25. Contemporary observers in a number of slave societies reported that this was an explicit calculation made by many planters. For ex-

amples see Franklin W. Knight, *Slave Society in Cuba during the Nineteenth Century* (Madison: University of Wisconsin Press, 1970), 75–76; C. R. Boxer, *The Golden Age of Brazil, 1695–1750: Growing Pains of a Colonial Society* (Berkeley: University of California Press, 1964), 173; and Gwendolyn Midlo Hall, *Social Control in Slave Plantation Societies: A Comparison of St. Domingue and Cuba* (Baltimore: Johns Hopkins Press, 1971), 24. But quite apart from the credibility of these observations or even the deliberate intentions of the planters themselves, the evidence is clear that except in North America, slave deaths exceeded slave births in every slave society as long as the Atlantic slave trade remained open. See Philip D. Curtin, *The Atlantic Slave Trade: A Census* (Madison: University of Wisconsin Press, 1969), 28–30.

26. Lecture of 17 March, *Lectures de M. Foucault.*

27. See Hugh Tinker, *A New System of Slavery: The Export of Indian Labour Overseas, 1830–1920* (London: Oxford University Press for the Institute of Race Relations, 1974).

28. This is powerfully argued in Ira Berlin, *Many Thousands Gone: The First Two Centuries of Slavery in North America* (Cambridge, Mass.: Harvard University Press, 1998); and Kathleen M. Brown, *Good Wives, Nasty Wenches, & Anxious Patriarchs: Gender, Race, and Power in Colonial Virginia* (Chapel Hill: University of North Carolina Press, 1996).

29. Martha Hodes, *White Women, Black Men: Illicit Sex in the Nineteenth-Century South* (New Haven: Yale University Press, 1997).

30. There are, of course, other possible linkages between gender, sexuality, race, and labor. Hannah Rosen has shown how the very notions of the public sphere, civic virtue, and citizenship articulated with gender and racial ideologies in "The Gender of Reconstruction: Rape, Race, and Citizenship in the Postemancipation South" (Ph.D. diss., University of Chicago, 1999).

31. I am grateful to Leora Auslander for suggesting this thematic linkage between the two eras.

32. J. H. Elliott, *Imperial Spain, 1469–1716* (London: Penguin, 1963), 110.

33. Norman Roth, *Conversos, Inquisition, and the Expulsion of the Jews from Spain* (Madison: University of Wisconsin Press, 1995).

34. This is far too complicated an issue to take on here, but suffice it

to say that my reading of the evidence convinces me that the expulsion was not only a determining moment in the development of racial thought and practice, but also one that reveals much about the ambiguous boundaries of racial phenomena, in this case the boundary between race and religion. For a sample of the conflicting literature on the expulsion, see Hannaford, *Race*, 105–126; Roth, *Conversos, Inquisition, and Expulsion;* and John Lynch, "Spain after the Expulsion," in *Spain and the Jews: The Sephardic Experience, 1492 and After,* ed. Elie Kedourie (London: Thames and Hudson, 1992), 140–161. For insights into how this played out in America, I am indebted to Maria Elena Martinez, "Space, Order, and Group Identities: Puebla de Los Angeles," in *The Collective and the Public in Latin America: Cultural Identities and Political Order* (Brighton, U.K.: Sussex Academic, forthcoming).

35. Goldberg, *Racist Culture,* 79.

36. Benedict Anderson, *Imagined Communities: Reflections on the Origins and Spread of Nationalism* (London: Verso, 1983).

37. "Nations do not make states and nationalism but the other way around"; Eric J. Hobsbawm, *Nations and Nationalism since 1780: Programme, Myth, Reality,* 2d ed. (Cambridge: Cambridge University Press, 1990), 10.

38. Leora Auslander, "Revolutionary Taste: Everyday Life and Politics in England, France, and America" (Manuscript, 1997); Etienne Balibar, "Racism and Nationalism," in *Race, Nation, Class: Ambiguous Identities,* ed. Etienne Balibar and Immanuel Wallerstein (London: Verso, 1991), 44–54.

39. Anderson, *Imagined Communities.*

40. Reginald Horsman, *Race and Manifest Destiny: The Origins of American Racial Anglo-Saxonism* (Cambridge, Mass.: Harvard University Press, 1981).

41. Jordan, *White over Black,* 24.

42. Auslander, "Revolutionary Taste."

43. Anderson, *Imagined Communities,* 129–140. In contrast, David Goldberg writes: "Nation has both a conceptual and social history intersecting with that of race. Originally used to refer to those who claimed to be of common birth or extended family (1584), the sense of nation simulated the early significance of race as lineage. The popular Enlightenment concern with national characteristics

often explicitly identified these characteristics racially"; *Racist Culture,* 78.

44. The relations of *conversos* to unconverted Jews were very complex. Indeed, some authors suggest the complicity of one or the other group in triggering the Inquisition that eventually led to expulsion; Elliott, *Imperial Spain;* Roth, *Conversos, Inquisition, and Expulsion.*

45. Gad J. Heuman, *Between Black and White: Race, Politics, and the Free Coloreds in Jamaica, 1791–1865* (Westport, Conn.: Greenwood Press, 1981), 6, 44–51.

46. David R. Roediger, *The Wages of Whiteness: Race and the Making of the American Working Class* (London: Verso, 1991); Matthew Frye Jacobson, *Whiteness of a Different Color: European Immigrants and the Alchemy of Race* (Cambridge, Mass.: Harvard University Press, 1998).

47. Alejandro de la Fuentes, *A Nation for All: Race, Inequality, and Politics in Cuba, 1900–2000* (Chapel Hill: University of North Carolina Press, 2000); Ada Ferrer, *Insurgent Cuba: Race, Nation, and Revolution, 1868–1898* (Chapel Hill: University of North Carolina Press, 1999).

48. Nancy Leys Stepans, *"The Hour of Eugenics": Race, Gender, and Nation in Latin America* (Ithaca: Cornell University Press, 1991).

49. Jacobson, *Whiteness of a Different Color;* and Ian F. Lopez, *White by Law: The Legal Construction of Race* (New York: New York University Presses, 1996).

50. David Montejano, *Anglos and Mexicans in the Making of Texas, 1836–1986* (Austin: University of Texas Press, 1987), 34–37, quotation p. 35.

51. Ibid., 36, 37.

52. Ibid., 41–51.

53. Ibid., 50, 84–85, 114–115; quotations pp. 7, 115.

54. Neil Foley, *The White Scourge: Mexicans, Blacks, and Poor Whites in Texas Cotton Culture* (Berkeley: University of California Press, 1997).

55. Ibid., 208.

56. Ibid., 209, 210.

57. Ira Berlin, *Slaves without Masters: The Free Negro in the Antebellum South* (New York: Pantheon, 1974), 131.

## 2. Race and Culture in a Consumer Society

1. My own initial effort to specify the link between such broad structures and everyday life and their implications for analyses of racism can be found in Thomas C. Holt, "Marking: Race, Race-making, and the Writing of History," *American Historical Review* 100 (February 1995): 1–20.

2. Among recent scholars Lizabeth Cohen has pioneered this thesis, but an earlier formulation of it can also be found in Du Bois's essays in *The Crisis* during the early 1930s, written as this consumption regime was taking shape. For Du Bois, see Thomas C. Holt, "The Political Uses of Alienation: W. E. B. Du Bois on Politics, Race, and Culture, 1903–1940," *American Quarterly* 42 (June 1990): 301–323. For Cohen, see "Citizens and Consumers in the Century of Mass Consumption," in *Material Politics: States, Consumers, and Political Culture,* ed. Martin Daunton and Matthew Hilton (Oxford: Berg, 2000); and *A Consumer's Republic: The Politics of Consumption in Postwar America* (New York: Alfred A. Knopf, forthcoming).

3. William Julius Wilson, *The Declining Significance of Race: Blacks and Changing American Institutions* (Chicago: University of Chicago Press, 1978).

4. David Harvey, *The Condition of Postmodernity: An Enquiry into the Origins of Cultural Change* (Oxford: Oxford University Press, 1989).

5. Susan Strasser, "Consumption," in *Encyclopedia of the United States in the Twentieth Century, Part 5, The Economy,* ed. Stanley Kutler (New York: Charles Scribners, 1996), 1017–35; and Stuart Ewen, *Captains of Consciousness: Advertising and the Social Roots of the Consumer Culture* (New York: McGraw-Hill, 1976).

6. Martha Olney, *Buy Now, Pay Later: Advertising, Credit, and Consumer Durables in the 1920s* (Chapel Hill: University of North Carolina Press, 1991).

7. Meg Jacobs, "The Politics of Purchasing Power: Political Economy, Consumption Politics, and State-Building, 1909–1959" (Ph.D. diss., University of Virginia, 1998).

8. Lizabeth Cohen, *Making a New Deal: Industrial Workers in Chicago, 1919–1939* (Cambridge: Cambridge University Press, 1990), 273–274.

9. Ibid., 289. Lawrence W. Levine describes a similar response among African Americans; "The Folklore of Industrial Society: Popular Culture and Its Audiences," *American Historical Review* 97 (December 1992): 1394.

10. The bailouts of major employers like Lockheed and Chrysler in the early years of the post-Fordist regime are well known. More recently capitalist speculators, like Long-Term Capital Management, have also sought the state's protection; "Hedge-Fund Withdrawal," *New York Times,* 9 September 1999. Similar responses by Germany's socialist government show that this is a feature of political economy rather than an idiosyncrasy of U.S. politics; Edmund L. Andrews, "Germany's Consensus Economy at Risk of Unraveling," *New York Times,* 26 November 1999.

11. August Meier and Elliott Rudwick, *Black Detroit and the Rise of the U. A. W.* (New York: Oxford University Press, 1979), 3–33. For a more general discussion of black employment in Detroit in this period, see Richard W. Thomas, *Life for Us Is What We Make It: Building Black Community in Detroit, 1915–1945* (Bloomington: Indiana University Press, 1992), 26–35.

12. Meier and Rudwick, *Black Detroit,* 9–11. Blacks constituted a substantial portion of the industry by the 1930s; ibid., 6.

13. For background and a narrative of the trial, see Thomas, *Building Black Community in Detroit,* 137–140; and David Allan Levine, *Internal Combustion: The Races in Detroit, 1915–1926* (Westport, Conn.: Greenwood Press, 1976), 158–198.

14. For examples of black press coverage, see "Racial Clash Seems Near: Blame KKK," *Houston Informer,* 26 September 1925; and "Residential Segregation," *Public Journal* (Philadelphia), 10 October 1925, Papers of the NAACP, Washington, D.C., Part 5, The Campaign against Residential Segregation, 1914–1953, Group I, Box D-86, Cases Supported, 1910–1940, microfilm reel 2, frames 975, 985.

15. "Arguments of Clarence Darrow in the case of Henry Sweet," May 11, 1926, in *People v. Sweet,* Recorders Court of Detroit, Michigan, Papers of the NAACP, Part 5, The Campaign against Residential Segregation, 1924–1955, Group I, Box D-87, Cases Supported, 1920–1940, microfilm reel 3, frames 5560–5683.

16. Thurgood Marshall, "Memorandum to the President of the United

States Concerning Racial Discrimination by the Federal Housing Administration," 1 February 1949, Papers of the NAACP, Part 5, The Campaign against Residential Segregation, 1914–1955, Group II, Box A-311, Housing, microfilm reel 7, frames 644–664; quotation from 661.

17. For exposition of this category, see James R. Barrett and David Roediger, "Inbetween Peoples: Race, Nationality, and the 'New Immigrant Working Class,'" *Journal of American Ethnic History* 16, no. 3 (Spring 1997): 3–44.

18. Theresa Mah, "Buying into the Middle Class: Residential Segregation and Racial Formation in the United States, 1920–1964" (Ph. D. diss., University of Chicago, 2000).

19. For examples of this line of thought, see an NAACP press briefing memo, which makes clear what in their view was at stake: "Negroes will be free to move into areas hitherto closed to them and it may be expected that Negroes of means and culture will be able to purchase and occupy homes suitable to their social and economic standing, while middle class Negroes will also be allowed to leave the narrow confines of the slum area and be gradually absorbed into areas occupied by other citizens of similar economic and social standing"; "Background Materials for Newspapers on Press Conference September 6, 1947," draft memo in Part 5, The Campaign against Residential Segregation, 1914–1955, Group II, Box B-133, Restrictive Covenants Cases, microfilm reel 22, frame 221. For a similar assessment of the *Sweet* decision by a prominent lawyer unsympathetic to the decision, see H. O. Weitschat, "What the Sweet Acquittal Means," NAACP Papers, Group I, Series D, Box D-87, Cases Supported, microfilm reel 3, frames 855–857.

20. Thomas J. Sugrue, *The Origins of the Urban Crisis: Race and Inequality in Postwar Detroit* (Princeton: Princeton University Press, 1996), 213, 254.

21. Ibid., 211–219. A survey of Detroit in 1985 is very revealing about how these connections between property, race, and self are made: "not being black is what constitutes being middle class; not living with blacks is what makes a neighborhood a decent place to live"; quoted in Thomas Bryne Edsall with Mary D. Edsall, "Race," *Atlantic Monthly* 267, no. 5 (May 1991), 56.

22. Sugrue, *Origins of the Urban Crisis,* 234–261.

23. See Thomas J. Sugrue, "Crabgrass-Roots Politics: Race, Rights, and the Reaction against Liberalism in the Urban North, 1940–1964," *Journal of American History* 82 (September 1995): 551–578; and Arnold R. Hirsch, "Massive Resistance in the Urban North: Trumbull Park, Chicago, 1953–1966," ibid., 522–550.

24. Lizabeth Cohen, "Citizens and Consumers."

25. Clifford Geertz, "Deep Play: Notes on the Balinese Cockfight" in *The Interpretation of Cultures: Selected Essays* (New York: Basic Books, 1973), 412–453, quotation p. 450..

26. Jill Dupont, " 'The Self in the Ring, the Self in Society': Boxing and American Culture from Jack Johnson to Joe Louis" (Ph.D. diss., University of Chicago, 2000), chap. 1.

27. Ibid., chap. 5.

28. For more on the film itself as well as the campaign to ban it, see Thomas Cripps, *Slow Fade to Black: The Negro in American Film, 1900–1942* (New York: Oxford University Press, 1977), 41–69.

29. Ibid., 52.

30. Ibid., 52–69.

31. Melvin Patrick Ely, *The Adventures of Amos 'n' Andy: A Social History of an American Phenomenon* (New York: Free Press, 1991).

32. George Lipsitz, *Time Passages: Collective Memory and American Popular Culture* (Minneapolis: University of Minnesota Press, 1990), 39–76.

33. Ely, *Amos 'n' Andy.*

34. Quoted in Laurie Beth Green, "Battling the Plantation Mentality: Consciousness, Culture, and the Politics of Race, Class, and Gender in Memphis, 1940–1968" (Ph.D. diss., University of Chicago, 1999), 241.

35. Laurie Mifflin, "N.A.A.C.P. Plans to Press for More Diverse TV Shows," *New York Times,* 13 July 1999; and Bernard Weinraub, "Stung by Criticism of Fall Shows, TV Networks Add Minority Roles," *New York Times,* 20 September 1999.

36. Laurie Green explores the fascinating impact of Memphis black radio generally on the evolving consciousness in black Memphis in the 1940s and specifically on the development of protests; "Battling the Plantation Mentality," 207–282. See also Kathy M. Newman, "The Forgotten Fifteen Million: Black Radio, the 'Negro Market,'

and the Civil Rights Movement," *Radical History Review* 76 (Winter 2000): 115–135.

37. Cohen, "Citizens and Consumers."

38. When I am traveling abroad, for example, and say that I am from Chicago, I am immediately identified with Michael Jordan and the Chicago Bulls. My experience is far from unique, of course. Other travelers report similar experiences from deep in Asia. For examples see Walter LaFeber, *Michael Jordan and the New Global Capitalism* (New York: W. W. Norton, 1999).

39. "The Value of the Press and Publicity in the Fight for Justice," address by Nahum Daniel Brascher at annual meeting of NAACP, Newark, N.J., 21 June 1922, Papers of the NAACP, Part 1, Minutes of the Board of Directors, 1909–1950, Group I, Series B. Box 5, Speeches, June 18–23, microfilm reel 8, frames 1134–54.

## 3. RACE, NATION, AND THE GLOBAL ECONOMY

1. The most dramatic of these were the "Don't Buy Where You Can't Work" boycotts that swept several northern cities in the 1930s. These were also among the first to combine consumer action with an explicitly economic agenda. For a study of one such movement, see Andor Skotnes, "'Buy Where You Can Work': Boycotting for Jobs in African-American Baltimore, 1933–1934," *Journal of Social History* 27 (Summer 1994): 735–761.

2. The earliest and most obvious example of such cross-purpose responses was, successive presidential proclamations to the contrary, the FHA's encouragement of credit procedures that promoted segregated housing. Another was the Justice Department's support of integration while the FBI systematically attacked social movements and their leaders.

3. Robert Korstad and Nelson Lichtenstein, "Opportunities Found and Lost: Labor, Radicals, and the Early Civil Rights Movement," *Journal of American History* 75 (1988): 786–811.

4. See, for example, Charles M. Payne, *I've Got the Light of Freedom: The Organizing Tradition and the Mississippi Freedom Struggle* (Berkeley: University of California Press, 1995).

5. Charles Payne, "Ella Baker and Models of Social Change," *Signs* 14

(Summer 1989): 885–899; Barbara Ransby, *Ella J. Baker and the Black Radical Tradition* (Chapel Hill: University of North Carolina Press, forthcoming).

6. See Walter A. Jackson, *Gunnar Myrdal and America's Conscience: Social Engineering and Racial Liberalism, 1938–1987* (Chapel Hill: University of North Carolina Press, 1990).

7. The Garland Fund never delivered most of the funds it promised. And SNCC workers worried—apparently with some reason—that accepting money from foundations might compromise them politically. On the 1930s initiative, see Mark V. Tushnet, *The NAACP's Legal Strategy against Segregated Education, 1925–1950* (Chapel Hill: University of North Carolina Press, 1987); on the 1960s, see Clayborne Carson, *In Struggle: SNCC and the Black Awakening of the 1960s* (Cambridge, Mass.: Harvard University Press, 1981), 38–42, 70.

8. See Herbert Hill, "Racism within Organized Labor: A Report of Five Years of the AFL-CIO, 1955–1960," *Journal of Negro Education* 30 (Spring 1961): 109–118; Philip S. Foner, *Organized Labor and the Black Worker, 1619–1981* (New York: International Publishers, 1981).

9. For a contemporary account of this racial opening among southern tobacco workers, see Ted Poston, "The Making of Mama Harris," *New Republic* 103, no. 194 (4 November 1940): 624–626. For a less sanguine scholarly account, see Delores E. Janiewski, *Sisterhood Denied: Race, Gender, and Class in a New South Community* (Philadelphia: Temple University Press, 1985).

10. Lizabeth Cohen, "Citizens and Consumers in the Century of Mass Consumption," in *Material Politics: States, Consumers, and Political Culture,* ed. Martin Daunton and Matthew Hilton (Oxford: Berg, 2000). For the complex and sharply disputed relations between the Civil Rights Movement and labor, see Michael K. Honey, *Southern Labor and Black Civil Rights: Organizing Memphis Workers* (Urbana: University of Illinois, 1993); Herbert Hill, "Lichtenstein's Fictions: Meany, Reuther and the 1964 Civil Rights Act," *New Politics* 7 (Summer 1998): 82–107; Laurie Beth Green, "Battling the Plantation Mentality: Consciousness, Culture, and the Politics of Race, Class, and Gender in Memphis, 1940–1968" (Ph.D. diss., University of Chicago, 1999).

11. Meg Jacobs, "The Politics of Purchasing Power: Political Economy, Consumption Politics, and State-Building, 1909–1959" (Ph.D. diss., University of Virginia, 1998).

12. August Meier and Elliott Rudwick, *Black Detroit and the Rise of the U. A. W.* (New York: Oxford University Press, 1979).

13. Gay W. Seidman, *Manufacturing Militance: Workers' Movements in Brazil and South Africa, 1970–1985* (Berkeley: University of California Press, 1994).

14. Green, "Battling the Plantation Mentality."

15. For a more narrowly focused analysis, see Thomas Byrne Edsall (with Mary D. Edsall), "Race," *Atlantic Monthly*, May 1991, 53–86.

16. Walter LaFeber points out other salient differences between multinational capital in the late nineteenth and early twentieth centuries and such firms today. First, whereas earlier companies—Standard Oil, Eastman Kodak, Singer (sewing machines), McCormick (harvesters)—made products largely with American labor and for American markets, today's multinational firms earn 80 percent of their revenues from overseas production. Four of every five bottles of Coca-Cola are sold abroad. Second, the earlier firms traded natural resources and industrial goods, while today's firms trade in "designs, technical knowledge, management techniques, and organizational innovations. The key to success was not so much the goods as it was knowledge: the quickly formulated and transferred engineering and marketing information, the control of advanced, rapidly changing technology (such as how to make computer software—or Air Jordans"; Walter LaFeber, *Michael Jordan and the New Global Capitalism* (New York: W. W. Norton, 1999), 55–57.

17. This description draws heavily upon the fascinating work of Saskia Sassen: *The Mobility of Labor and Capital: A Study in International Investment and Labor Flow* (Cambridge: Cambridge University Press, 1988), 1–3; and *The Global City: New York, London, Tokyo* (Princeton: Princeton University Press, 1991), 9, 62–63, 83.

18. Sassen, *The Global City;* idem, *Mobility of Labor and Capital,* 52–53, quotation on 187.

19. Sassen, *Mobility of Labor and Capital,* 24

20. Sassen, *The Global City,* 244.

21. Moreover, such comparisons, historically and analytically suspect,

always carry the message that blacks should pull up their socks and work like the immigrants.

22. Perhaps nowhere is this problem more starkly evident and debated in such unapologetically racist terms than in contemporary Japan. See, for example, Howard W. French, "Still Wary of Outsiders, Japan Expects Immigration Boom," *New York Times,* 14 March 2000.

23. David Harvey, *The Condition of Postmodernity: An Enquiry into the Origins of Cultural Change* (Oxford: Basil Blackwell, 1989), vii.

24. The story is, of course, even more complex. First, this new form of capital ownership relies on computer technology to "package" financial instruments (bundles) for sale and purchase that are really shards, not of the original bonds or stocks, but of *options* to buy or sell bonds and stocks at a future date, price, and/or under specified conditions. Apparently only a few financiers actually understand what these entities are or how they will behave. The definition offered by one financial house suggests its highly contingent and variable nature. "A derivative instrument generally consists of, is based upon, or exhibits characteristics similar to *options* or *forward contracts.* Options and forward contracts are considered to be the basic 'building blocks' of derivatives . . . Diverse types of derivatives may be created by combining options and forward contracts in different ways, and by applying these structures to a wide range of underlying assets"; *The Strong Income Funds: Investment Information and Prospectus,* March 1997, 1–22.

25. Eric J. Hobsbawm, *Nations and Nationalism since 1780: Programme, Myth, Reality,* 2d ed. (Cambridge: Cambridge University Press, 1990).

26. An interesting fact in this regard: "Of the hundred largest economic units in the world of the 1980s, only half were nations. The other half were individual corporations"; LaFeber, *Michael Jordan and the New Global Capitalism,* 57.

27. Zygmunt Bauman, "Soil, Blood and Identity," *Sociological Review* 40, no. 4 (1992): 690.

28. Among the many examples recently published in the daily press, see Robert E. Stevenson, "Greenspan Defends Fed's Rate Policy," *New York Times,* 9 May 1997, D1, D13. In the late 1990s many economic observers postulated that the Philips Curve on which this

theory was based had become obsolescent, that a "new economy" had taken hold which allowed for extraordinarily low unemployment without sparking inflation. Other analysts are much more cautious in judging the validity or longevity of the change. And in any event the basic policy has not changed, only the levels at which it is invoked: the Fed still expects that too great a labor demand will spark inflation; the only question is when. For reasons I will make clear, even the new economy is built on the services of a "reserve army" of labor—sweatshop workers and offshore sources.

29. See Bart Landry, *The New Black Middle Class* (Berkeley: University of California Press, 1987), 141–155.

30. For an entrée into the literature on so-called underclass debate, see William Julius Wilson, *The Truly Disadvantaged: The Inner City, the Underclass, and Public Policy* (Chicago: University of Chicago Press, 1987); and Michael B. Katz, ed., *The "Underclass" Debate: Views from History* (Princeton: Princeton University Press, 1993). For an exploration of these issues in the context of economic globalization, see Clarence Lusane, *Race in the Global Era: African-Americans in the Millennium* (Boston: South End Press, 1997).

31. Mike Davis, *City of Quartz: Excavating the Future in Los Angeles* (London: Vintage, 1990).

32. Sassen, *The Global City*, 317.

33. LaFeber, *Michael Jordan and the New Global Capitalism*, 18.

34. I am indebted here to insights in Leora Auslander, *Taste and Power: Furnishing Modern France* (Berkeley: University of California Press, 1996), 415–425.

35. For a similar argument, though independently developed and differently framed from this one, see Anne Norton, *A Republic of Signs: Liberal Theory and American Popular Culture* (Chicago: University of Chicago Press, 1993), esp. 47–122.

36. See Harvey, *Condition of Postmodernity*.

37. For Suchard and Grace Jones images, see Raymond Bachollet, Jean-Barthélemi Debost, Anne-Claude Lelieur, and Marie-Christine Peyrière, *Négripub: L'image des Noirs dans la publicité* (Paris: Somogy, 1992).

38. LaFeber, *Michael Jordan and the New Global Capitalism*.

39. Ibid., 24.

40. In 1992 Nike's overseas sales totaled $1 billion, of which 15 percent

was in Asia, 75 percent in Europe, and 10 percent in Canada and Latin America; ibid., 104–106, 108.

41. Ibid., 63, 107.

42. Quoted in ibid., 85.

43. Oscar Robinson, one of Jordan's superstar predecessors, was not offered a single endorsement contract until he had been a professional for four years, and then only to endorse a basketball; ibid., 45.

44. Blacks were not accepted into pro basketball until the 1949–50 season, but by the 1980s they accounted for 80 percent of starting players. Their growing visibility led Martin Kane to publish an article in *Sports Illustrated* in 1971, claiming that biology rather than socieconomics explained black dominance of sport; ibid., 46.

45. For example, see George M. Frederickson, *The Arrogance of Race: Historical Perspectives on Slavery, Racism, and Social Inequality* (Middletown, Conn.: Wesleyan University Press, 1988), 189.

46. Henry Louis Gates Jr., "The Powell Perplex," in *Thirteen Ways of Looking at a Black Man* (New York: Vintage, 1998), 82–83.

47. Edsall, "Race," 53.

48. Bauman is eloquent on the modern condition in "Soil, Blood and Identity," 689–698.

49. Among the many examples of this phenomenon was the killing of a black youth in Maryland in May 1989 for his Air Jordans. Meanwhile the odds of a black youth in his twenties actually playing in the NBA was 135,800 to 1. LaFeber, *Michael Jordan and the New Global Capitalism*, 91.

50. Kenneth B. Noble, "Thai Workers Are Set Free in California," *New York Times*, 4 August 1995, A1. See also related stories in *New York Times*, 6 February 1995, A1; 12 March 1995, 1.1; 5 August 1995, 1.6; 14 December 1997.